Children and young people as ...

DA
ON

ovim
izard
lows
ed by
llows
trong

ISBN 0 902 817 56 6

Published by the National Children's Bureau
8 Wakley Street
London EC1V 7QE
Telephone 071 278 9441

Cover illustration by Anne Bristow
Design, typesetting and artwork by Lasso 071-272 9141
Printed by Russell Press 0602 784505

The National Children's Bureau was established as a registered charity in 1963. Our purpose is to identify and promote the interests of all children and young people and to improve their status in a diverse and multiracial society.

We work closely with professionals and policy makers to improve the lives of all children but especially children under five, those affected by family instability and children with special needs or disabilities.

We collect and disseminate information about children and promote good practice in children's services through research, policy and practice development, publications, seminars, training and an extensive library and information service.

Contents

■

Foreword

■

I am delighted to introduce this collection of papers on children and young people as abusers. For some time, ChildLine has been concerned about both the children who tell us their abuser was another young person and the children who contact us to tell us that they themselves are abusing others. We were happy to join with the Training Advisory Group on Child Sexual Abuse (TAGOSAC) in holding a consultative seminar in March 1990 to bring together professionals from all the disciplines working in this field so that we could establish a baseline of experience and assess the best ways to carry this work forward. Dr Arnon Bentovim kindly agreed to present a paper reflecting research and experience both in the UK and in the USA. Since the seminar, he has had the opportunity to expand the material he presented and we are pleased to include his revised paper as the major contribution to this publication. Dr Eileen Vizard also agreed to prepare a paper based on her contribution to the seminar. Dr Vizard's paper looks at the ways in which themes and responses to sexual abuse have emerged over the past decade, and suggests some of the key issues in working with children and young people as abusers which will have to be addressed in order to develop a coherent response in this area of work. Anne Hollows has drawn together much of the content of the workshop sessions from the seminar in two sections; first, an assessment of the current issues and practice in this field of work and second, the perspectives of practitioners on the developments which they would like to see in the future. Anne Hollows, with Helen Armstrong who organised the conference, developed the content of the final plenary session of the seminar into an Agenda for Action.

We hope that the impetus which was achieved at the seminar, together with the interest generated by this publication, will be carried forward into clear responses by all the agencies involved in meeting the challenge of this problem.

Valerie Howarth
Director, ChildLine

The contributors

Arnon Bentovim is Consultant Child Psychiatrist at Great Ormond Street Hospital and the Tavistock Clinic.

Eileen Vizard is Consultant Child Psychiatrist at the Tavistock Clinic.

Anne Hollows is Senior Development Officer in the Child Abuse Training Unit at the National Children's Bureau.

Introduction

■

ANNE HOLLOWS

In the midst of all the uncertainty surrounding the sexual abuse of children, increasing concern is being registered that the perpetrators of sexual abuse may themselves be children and young people. This concern has developed from two distinct sources. First there is the evidence of teachers, carers, psychiatrists, social workers and others who observe behaviour of, and among, children. Second, there is the evidence from studies of adult abusers, a significant number of whom claim histories of abusing behaviour going back into their own childhood.

A little over a year ago, a consultative conference was convened at the National Children's Bureau to discuss the issue of children and young people who sexually abuse others. More than 80 participants attended the conference, reflecting varied experience in this area of work. For some, it was the first opportunity to share their experience, their anxieties, their dilemmas and their achievements with a community of trusting professionals. For others, the conference provided the challenge to explore the potential for new developments both in resources and in generating a wider awareness of the problem.

The period since the conference has been one of hectic activity in preparation for legislative changes affecting the legal context of work with children. This has been interspersed by several well publicised cases of suspected abuse. The prevailing view is that, even more than was previously thought, the investigation of child abuse must be carefully paced. At the same time there has been greater interest in the issue of treatment and prevention of abuse; in the understanding that abusers are in many cases addicted to their behaviour and that they urgently require treatment to break their behaviour patterns.

Overall, however, the prevalence of child sexual abuse is still uncertain and knowledge about the effectiveness of treatment interventions with abused and abuser alike is only beginning to develop. Indeed, it may well be a generation before the consequences of abuse on their adult lives can be assessed with confidence for today's abused children.

Set among these uncertainties, the concept of the sexual abuse of one child by another is almost too difficult to bear. It is hard enough when the abusing child is an adolescent, almost an adult, but almost beyond belief where the abusing child is very young. It is not surprising that many of those attending the conference have had to battle against the disbelief and denial of the problem among their colleagues, their managers and their friends.

Information from professionals confirms that many of the children who display inappropriate sexual behaviour towards other children will themselves have been the victims of some kind of abuse; probably, but not exclusively, sexual abuse. In a society which is still stumbling in its attempts to respond appropriately to suspicions of sexual abuse, and where treatment and therapeutic facilities for children who have been abused are still limited, this fusion of victim and victimiser in the same child poses massive problems of response.

Added to this there is the issue of definition of abuse. Can a child as young as three or four years be said to have the necessary intent to 'abuse'? In whose judgement is an act abusive? Where do we draw the line between experimentation and abuse? And where do we draw lines about age-appropriate behaviour? Above all, how do we, as professionals from a range of disciplines working with children, respond to the individual child and family in this situation?

Experience in America has recognised for some time the existence of children whose sexual behaviour towards other children is inappropriate and damaging. Work has been undertaken to explain the phenomenon and programmes have been developed to respond to the children involved. All of this is helpful guidance in the process of developing a response in the UK which recognises and works within the framework of existing child welfare services.

The Training Advisory Group on Sexually Abused Children, together with the Child Abuse Training Unit at the National Children's Bureau and ChildLine, hoped that the conference in spring 1990 would be a starting point for concerted action in the UK. This publication records the content of that conference, with Arnon Bentovim's keynote paper in an expanded form. It includes an analysis of the key issues raised at the seminar and develops an agenda for action, aimed at policy makers locally and nationally.

During the time which has elapsed since the conference, media attention on child abuse has concentrated on the investigation process surrounding child abuse, and the importance of making full and thorough enquiries. Although there have been reported instances of sexual assault by school pupils there has, as yet, been little attention paid to the issue of children who abuse other children, outside of the professional journals in this area. Concern within and between agencies is rising however. Enquiries to the Child Abuse Training Unit on this subject have increased and are coming from agencies outside the mainstream child welfare field. We hope that this publication will attract a wider range and span of attention to the issue.

In a recent case involving a seven-year-old girl, it became apparent that the symptoms of abuse were the result of sibling abuse, her sibling having himself been abused by a school friend. The school friend had been abused by his father. In this case a number of factors in a preliminary social assessment suggested, at the pre-investigation stage, that the girl's stepfather was the most likely abuser; no-one anticipated the eventual outcome. Increasing awareness that children can and do abuse other children and increasing knowledge of the potential responses to such abuse will help to protect all children from becoming part of a damaging web of abusive behaviour where the victim all too often develops the role of victimiser.

Children and young people as abusers

■

DR ARNON BENTOVIM

Introduction

There has been a rising concern about children and young people as abusers in recent years. This was first identified in North America and has more recently given cause for concern in the United Kingdom.

Kempe (Kempe, 1979) drew attention to the sequence of recognition of different forms of abuse within the community. If we take sexual abuse as a specific form of abuse, we see a similar sequence. Initially we focused on children and young people who had been abused, girls initially, then boys; very young children as well as children and adolescents. Most recently we have focused on the abuser, men, women and now children and young people. There has been an increasing awareness that abuse takes place within the context of trusted relationships, rather than by strangers.

Once there is an appreciation of the extent of abuse in the community and appropriate treatment is provided for those who have been abused (Bentovim *et al*, 1988), the next pressing concern is to help those who abuse. It has rapidly become clear that imprisonment and separation of the abuser from the family is no guarantee that they will not resume this behaviour at a later date. It is essential to understand more about abusers, to find out who they are, and what are the factors that led to their abusive behaviour. Only then will it be possible to devise appropriate treatment strategies.

Definitions

In most official publications the Schecter and Roberge definition of sexual abuse is recognised as the basic definition of such abuse (Schecter and Roberge, 1976), that is 'the involvement of dependent, developmentally immature children and adolescents in sexual activities they do not truly comprehend, to which they are unable to give informed consent and which violate the social taboos of family roles'. This definition, of course, does not in any way define who the abuser is. It is a definition which focuses on the child or young person abused. There is an implication that the concern is for dependent individuals. This in turn implies that the abuser is somebody on whom the child or young person is dependent, which means that the abuser has to be seen as a significantly older person, basically, an adult. A gap of five years is usually accepted as the age difference which defines abusive behaviour.

Other definitions also focus on the child, for example, the definition of Mrazek *et al* (1981) which included concern about the physical abusive activities focused around the genital areas, other forms of activity which involve genital contact, and other sexualised activities. It is possible to be more precise about these activities, leading to a definition which would include the following:

- pseudo-educative contact, fondling of genitals, masturbation of child, masturbation of adult, oral/genital contact, simulated sexual intercourse, vaginal intercourse, and anal intercourse;
- all forms of inappropriate/sexualised contact with a child;
- child pornography;
- prostitution.

This form of definition was used by Bentovim *et al* (1987) as a way of defining the abusive experiences of a series of children. These are all definitions by the act itself, and again do not define by the action of the perpetrator. It is possible to think of acts by perpetrators as acts which give them a sexual response, but this is far more difficult to define or recognise.

Johnson (1988), Johnson and Berry (1989) and Johnson (1989) have published a series of papers on children under the age of 12 who are abusive. They attempt to distinguish between appropriate exploration in childhood, and abusive behaviour in childhood. Appropriate exploration is defined as 'children or young people of a similar age and size who are basically involved in information gathering. Exploration is visual or tactile, and of limited duration'. 'Abusive behaviour is different in character, it is impulsive, has a compulsive quality to it, uses aggression and force. Coercion is used, and an exploitation of the authority of an older over a younger child to obtain participation. Fingers, penises, tongues, or objects are used to penetrate forcefully, at times causing physical damage'. The usual age gap which is seen as abusive is around five years, but Johnson puts forward a view that an age gap of two years may well represent a significant difference in childhood. There is also a clear difference in effect between abusive behaviour and appropriate exploration. The former is more likely to be intense, preoccupied and involved.

Such differences are qualitatively quite striking and although the number of subjects in each series reported by Johnson is small, they do represent significant observation of a phenomenon within the community which had elsewhere been described as explorative rather than potentially abusive. There have been other accounts of strikingly sexually abusive actions by young children. For instance, Chasnoff *et al* (1986), Friedrich (1988) and Yates (1982) described children whose sexual activities had a driven, compulsive quality.

Sexually abusive behaviour by adolescents, once they have entered puberty, with younger children has a closer identity to abuse noted by adults and the age gap is far more likely to be five years or more.

This definition immediately raises issues of the extent, knowledge and patterns of sexual behaviour within childhood and adolescence. Smith and Grocke (1990) are in the process of completing a study on self-concepts and cognitions about sexuality in abused and non abused children. They are exploring the extent of detailed knowledge of sexual issues amongst younger children, the proportion of children who touch their parents' genitalia, those who have seen explicit videos or witnessed intercourse, and whether there are significant differences amongst children in terms of the degree of knowledge. They are also exploring cultural differences between social class groups in terms of the amount of restrictiveness of practices and attitudes about sexuality. This information, when published, will provide an important context for sexual actions of children and young people, since information about children and young people's 'normal' sexual activities is very limited (Rosenfeld *et al*, 1986 and 1987).

Frequency of abusive behaviour in children and young people

There has been particular concern in recent years about adolescents who are abusive, particularly in North America. However, we have very little information from population studies to understand or even know what the pattern of abusive behaviour is in adolescence and even less in children. Two major retrospective surveys of adults concerning abusive experiences in childhood, by Finkelhor (1979) and Russell (1983), give information on the ages of perpetrators and their relationships. Significantly such adults are not asked about their own abusive activities – clearly outside an ethical remit in normal population studies.

Finkelhor's classic study of the abusive experience of college students found that 19.2% of women and 8.6% of men had been sexually abused in childhood. What we have been less aware of in this study is the age of the perpetrator. Among both men and women, 1 in 4 described abuse by an adolescent partner.

When intra familial abuse was examined the largest amount of incestuous contact occurred between partners of the same generation: brothers, sisters and cousins. Ten per cent of the intra familial abuse involved cross-generational liaisons whereas 90% involved liaisons within the same generation. Brothers were sexually involved with older brothers almost as often as they were with sisters, and sisters reported a fair number of homosexual experiences too. Fifteen per cent of the abused girls and 10% of the boys had such sexual experiences.

Finkelhor also reported that 30% of sibling incest was said to take place with force, or threat of force. This was not limited to partners who were much older, force and coercion being reported between siblings who were fairly close in age. Finkelhor also concluded that experiences were much more negative for a child when force was involved, and the older the partner the more unpleasant the experience. There were some differences described between boys and girls, so that girls who had abusive experiences with adolescents found them as traumatic as those who had experiences with adults. Boys expressed less displeasure with adolescent partners.

Russell (1983) in a comprehensive and detailed study of 930 women in North America found a high prevalence of sexual abuse amongst these women. About a half (54%) reported at least one experience of abuse either within or outside the family before the age of 18, and many of these experiences were reported as having occurred before the age of 14. When she looked at those women who had been abused within the family, it was reported that the 930 women reported abuse by their fathers, and 46 (4.9%) reported abuse by their uncles. Looking at abuse within the same generation, 20 (2.2%) of the women reported that their brothers had abused them, and 28 (3%) reported that their first cousins had abused them. It was striking that in Russell's study only three (0.3%) reported abuse by a sister. Another important finding from her study was looking at the seriousness of the abuse. She compared the abuse reported by brothers or half brothers to the abuse experienced outside the family. A quarter (27%) of the women described that the abuse by their brother or half brother was very serious, including violence, attempts at intercourse penetration; two thirds (62%) described their abuse as serious, and only 12% reported the abuse as being in the least serious category. Thus being in close contact with a sibling or half sibling meant that there were opportunities for sexual contact of an increasingly abusive and violent nature to be perpetrated. By comparison non-family abuse was far more likely to be described as less serious. Obviously there is a small amount of extra-familial abuse which is extremely serious, but it highlights the fact that the majority of serious abuse occurs within a known context.

Briere and Runtz (1989) in a study of male university students found an unexpectedly high rate of sexual interest in children. 21% of subjects reported sexual attraction to some small children. 9% described sexual fantasies involving children, 5% admitted to having masturbated to such fantasies, and 7% indicated some likelihood of having sex with a child if they could avoid detection and punishment. Such sexual interests were associated with a number of negative early sexual experiences, sexual conflicts and attitudes supportive of sexual dominance over women, and therefore patriarchal views. It would of course be interesting to know whether such young people had themselves been abused and whether their attitudes had begun earlier in adolescence or had occurred relatively more recently.

While such studies in the USA indicate the serious nature of abuse within the same generation, and within children and young people's experiences and attitudes, there is little work in the UK to examine this phenomenon. Baker and Duncan's (1987) study does not break down the perpetrator in terms of age.

The incidence of abusive behaviour in children and young people – clinical studies of abuse

Davies and Leitenberg (1987), in an extensive review of sexual offences committed by adolescents, noted that there had been little distinction of such offences from adult offenders because of the belief that few sexual offences of any serious consequence were perpetrated by adolescents (Becker and Abel, 1984). However, they noted that arrest statistics and victim surveys in the United States indicated that about 20% of all rapes and about 30–50% of all cases of child sexual abuse could be attributed to adolescent offenders (Brown *et al*, 1984). In the UK, 34% of males convicted for rape in 1985 were under 21 (Lloyd and Walmsley, 1989).

In addition, approximately 50% of adult sex offenders report that their first sexual offence occurred during adolescence (Abel *et al*, 1988, Gebhard *et al*, 1965, Groth *et al*, 1987). Many such future offenders described arousal to children when they were as young as the age of twelve. Although these figures do not imply that 50% of adolescent abusers go on to become adult perpetrators, certainly the implications are that sexually abusive activities by adolescents do need to be taken seriously as there may well be serious longer term consequences.

Although it might appear that many sexual abusers in adolescence are arrested and charged, Davies and Leitenberg (1987) conclude that such reporting, for instance of rapes or sexual victimisation, are the minority of complaints rather than representing all. Victims and families may be reluctant to report such activities because the offender is so young and known to the family. They may be considered insignificant or experimentation and therefore not requiring prosecution.

Ageton (1983) surveyed a normative and nationally representative sample of 863 male adolescents between thirteen and nineteen, aiming to obtain information on attempted or completed 'sexual assaults'. Between 4–8% indicated that they had been abusive, but sexual assaults or coercive sexual acts were defined as ranging from verbal pressure to use of a weapon. It may be that verbal pressure represents no more than unsuccessful attempts by boys to persuade their girl-friends to engage in intercourse. Thus this study, which seems to indicate a very high level of assaultative behaviour, may not be accurate enough in its means of analysis to sort out patterns of adolescent behaviour.

There have been some smaller scale studies of sibling and cousin incest (Smith and Israel, 1987, and de Jong, 1989). The perpetrators in their series were between the ages of thirteen and sixteen and victims between six and nine. The studies on young children (Johnson, 1988, 1989; Cantwell, 1988; Chasnoff *et al*, 1986) which focused on even younger children as abusers, described perpetrators between six and nine, and victims between three and four and a half or even younger.

In Johnson's series of 47 boy perpetrators, 23 involved sibling incest, and 12 of these abused younger brothers. In Smith and Israel's series there were five female and 20 male perpetrators including both children and adolescents. Their victims were overwhelmingly female. In de Jong's series (1989), victims were again overwhelmingly girls, while cousins were twice as likely to abuse a boy relative as a girl.

Generally speaking the results of surveys indicate that adolescent perpetrators abuse boys as much as they do girls. In our own recent research 24% of the abusers referred to a clinical child sexual abuse treatment project were young people, and 18% of the abusers were brothers of their victims. Abuse by young people of a serious nature is seen to be an increasingly recognised phenomenon which requires clinical attention.

Clinical example of a sibling abuse

An illustration of the sort of case which has been referred is a twelve-year-old sister abused by her older brother aged fourteen at referral. In our assessment meeting, carried out jointly with a social worker, we heard something of the concerns. Hetty was seen with her mother, she was extremely unhappy and distressed and we learned that she had begun to tell her mother about the abuse when they were on holiday. The abuse had been continuing for about two years, from when she was ten and her brother, Dan, was twelve. Dan had been lying on top of her, 'french' kissing her – that is kissing inside the mouth – and later this had progressed to trying to have intercourse with Hetty. We learned that he had pushed his fingers into her vagina on a number of occasions and also that at an earlier stage her mother had noticed that Dan was very interested in his sister's genitals. She had said quite clearly that this was not acceptable. The mother told us that she had faced Dan with Hetty's allegations earlier but he had denied his actions. The mother told us that she herself was unsure whether there had been abuse at all, and whether it might be a fantasy because she felt she had been present on some occasions when her daughter had alleged abuse had occurred, for example on holiday when Dan and Hetty had shared a room, and she had not been aware of anything untoward.

The girl described flashbacks in the form of nightmares, when she found herself thinking of the abuse episodes. She also described times in school when older girls had forcefully undressed her on a school holiday and shut her in a room. She was quite confused about the flashbacks from this episode as well as the abuse by her brother. She told us that she had partly not spoken about the episodes because she was worried about her father's physical illnesses which he had sustained the previous year. She did not describe abuse by any other person, although she indicated she was quite anxious about her father's shouting at her, and his bad temper.

Initially when we later talked to the boy and his father, we learned that he had some asthma, and also that his growth had been very slow. He said that he had not really started developing and he said defensively that he was not worried about himself; we got, however, a clear picture of his concerns about his growth. He said he got erections, and that he masturbated about grown-up women, not younger girls. He categorically denied that he had been abusive to his sister, and we had to challenge him by asking him was he happy for us to treat his sister as a compulsive liar, and in need of treatment. We persisted in our approach and he became distressed and tearful, and later was able to say that what his sister said was in fact true. He was able to make an initial somewhat stilted apology to his sister, but sufficient to enable us to plan treatment for the family which included a group for both sister and brother, as well as for the parents, with some family meetings associated. There was evidence of a very strained marital situation.

The boy was away in boarding school at this time so there was no immediate protective issue although the whole question of holiday periods needed careful thought and planning.

It is clear that the girl in this case was anxious. She described flashbacks, distress and unhappiness and she did not like her brother's forcing her or threatening her. She told us if she spoke he would kill her. She showed clear evidence of a post traumatic state.

Finkelhor (1979) in his retrospective research attempted to develop a traumatic index in relationship to adolescent abusers. McLeer *et al* (1988) noted in a retrospective study that 20.7% of an inpatient group who had been abused sexually described post traumatic states when reviewed retrospectively. They reported a small prospective study and where the father was the abuser, 75% (12) described post-traumatic reactions. Seventy-five per cent (8) described post traumatic states as a result of abuse by a trusted adult, but 0% of six described post traumatic symptoms as a result of abuse by an older child. This is an indication of how limited is the amount of information we have currently about the abusive effects of sexual abuse by children and older and young people on other children. Further research is very much required in this area.

The traumatic model to understand the nature of abuse and its effects

The most helpful model to understand the effects of abuse is the traumagenic model.

Figure 1 shows a simplified view of traumatic and abusive effects. At the top of the cycle, abusive acts lead to overwhelming, affective responses, which in turn lead to unbearable levels of anxiety and helplessness. These become unbearable, and there is no room for them to be accommodated in experience. Thus such responses are deleted and create what Bentovim and Kinston (1990) have described as a 'hole in the mind'. Instead a whole series of defensive actions and reactions occur in place of thought. These can take a variety of forms and may lead to patterns of victim behaviour, or repetitive actions and recreations which in turn lead to further abusive acts, either in relationship to the same or other abusers, or through abuse of others. The compulsion to act rather than experience and digest, is a characteristic of both abusers and the abused. Traumatic patterns of dissociation, and addictive repetition of abuse is a characteristic phenomenon which occurs in the face of unbearable levels of anxiety and helplessness.

Figure 1

Mechanisms leading to traumatic effects

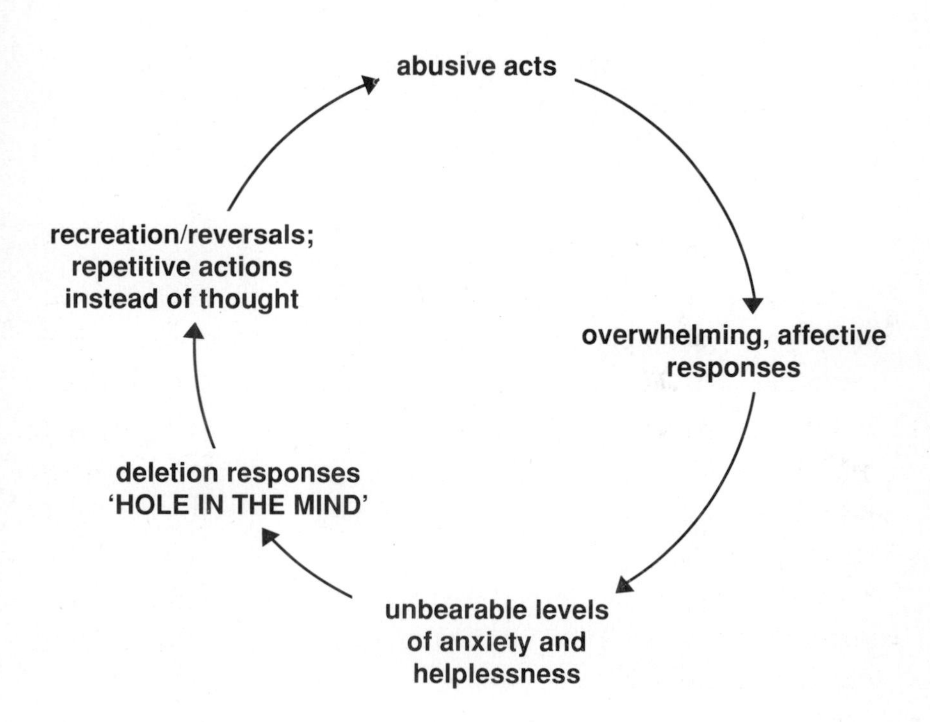

Specific applications of traumatic patterns – Finkelhor's traumagenic dynamics

Finkelhor's notions of traumagenic dynamics (Finkelhor and Browne, 1986 and Finkelhor, 1988) have been extremely helpful in understanding the phenomenon reactions to sexual abuse and he has described them under four basic headings:

- Traumatic Sexualisation
- Powerlessness
- Betrayal
- Stigmatisation Traumatic Sexualisation.

Traumatic sexualisation

Figure 2 recasts Finkelhor's notion of traumatic sexualisation into an interactive frame. He describes traumatic sexualisation as arising out of the rewarding of inappropriate responses, negative conditioning and an identification with victim or aggressor roles and activities. This leads into an interactive pattern which moves from avoidance and deletion phenomena, and various forms of recreations through identification with the activity through victim or perpetrator patterns of behaving. At one point there would be response through aversion, flashbacks of abusive acts, fears, and avoidance of contexts reminiscent of the abuse. There might then be episodes of sexual preoccupations and activities, leading to sexualising other children, or being reabused, which again triggers further aversions, flashbacks and phobias. Pynoos and Eth (1985), as well as describing cognitive flashbacks, have described the interesting phenomena of behavioural flashbacks, patterns of behaviour which are recreative of the original abusive acts, or perhaps the defensive process which is evoked to deal with the act.

Figure 2

Traumatic sexualisation

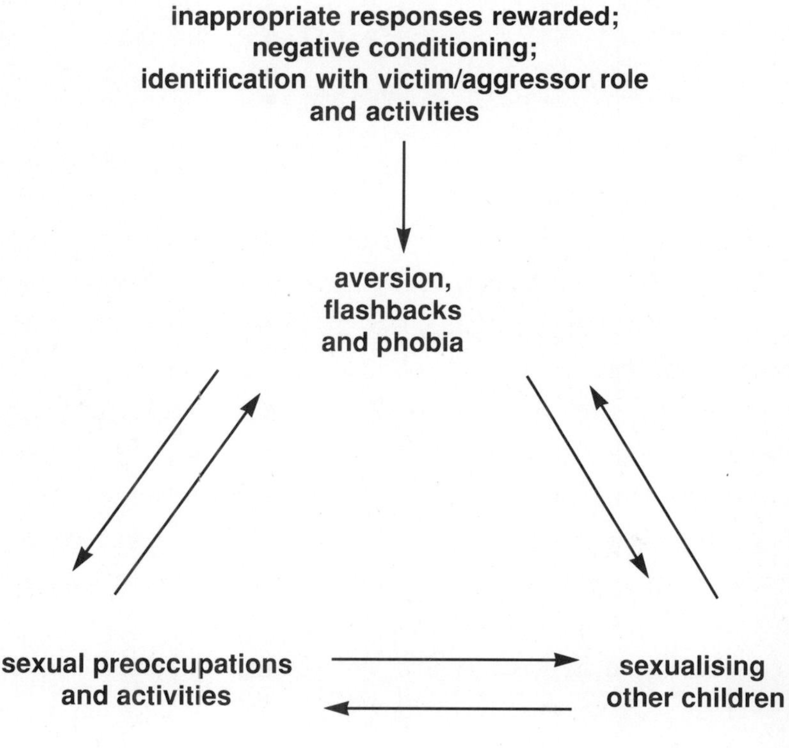

inappropriate responses rewarded;
negative conditioning;
identification with victim/aggressor role
and activities

aversion,
flashbacks
and phobia

sexual preoccupations
and activities

sexualising
other children

This is illustrated in an observation of a four and a half-year-old girl. She was placed in care of a foster parent when her drug abusing mother had left her alone in the flat with her younger siblings. Within the foster family she began to be very sexualised in her pattern of play with other children living in the foster family and also with the foster parents. When she was seen for an assessment interview and left with the anatomic dolls undressed, a typical pattern of behaviour with the dolls was observed. She was in the room with two social workers who were encouraging her to play with the dolls.

She initially showed an aversion to the dolls and said she wanted to put their clothes on, she was encouraged to play and it was noted that there was a 'flash' of response on her part. She examined the male doll's penis, pulled it and then picked up the doll saying forcefully 'There's a winkie coming'. She placed the doll on top of the child doll, squashed their genitals together, picked them both up and then made some obvious orgiastic sounding noises as she rubbed them violently together. Then suddenly the episode seemed to terminate, she put them down, turned away and went to another part of the room.

One could see a cycle of sexualised behaviour breaking through, given a context which reminded her of her original abuse. The action was initiated after some resistance and then terminated. It may well be that similar patterns are enacted between children who have been abused, given the high incidence of sexualisation as a behavioural response to sexual abuse. This may play a part in terms of sexualising other children, and initiating potentially abusive behaviour.

It is of interest to note that in Johnson's work 100% of her series of girls who abused had been abused themselves. This is a common experience; in our own clinical series (Bentovim *et al*, 1987) although only 5% of women abused, almost all had been universally abused themselves. [See Fehrenbach and Monasterky's (1988) survey.] It has been noted clinically that modes of inducing compliance between young people and children, specific sexual acts and even the age differences appear to be patterned after the original incident.

A broad view of studies of young people who have abused indicates the high percentage of these young people who had been abused in their own childhood. In Abel *et al*'s study (1988) 49% indicated that they had been abused in childhood. Becker (1988) and Fehrenbach *et al* (1986) found rates of 19%, Smith and Israel (1987) noted 52% of sibling perpetrators who had previously been abused, Johnson (1988) found 49% of her male child perpetrators had been abused, and Longo (1982) reported 47% had been abused.

One may conclude that the traumatic sexualisation effect is an important contributory, but probably not a necessary factor, in the development of subsequent abusive behaviour. The implications, however, are that a child referred because of concerns about sexually abusive behaviour should be assessed for possible abuse themselves.

Powerlessness

The second major traumagenic dynamic which Finkelhor has described as a result of sexual abuse is powerlessness. (Figure 3)

Powerlessness occurs as the result of invasion of the body giving a sense of vulnerability, absence of protection from someone who should be seen as a caring figure, repeated fear and a sense of helplessness. This results in an interactive process whereby the feeling state of fear, anxiety, inability to control events may trigger learning difficulties, a sense of despair, a low efficacy; alternatively a response of a need to control, dominate, and to adopt an aggressive and abusive stance may result. The figure indicates that this is an interactive process whereby one state leads to a response reaction which in turn leads back to the other state. Linked with the previous dynamic of traumatic sexualisa-

Figure 3

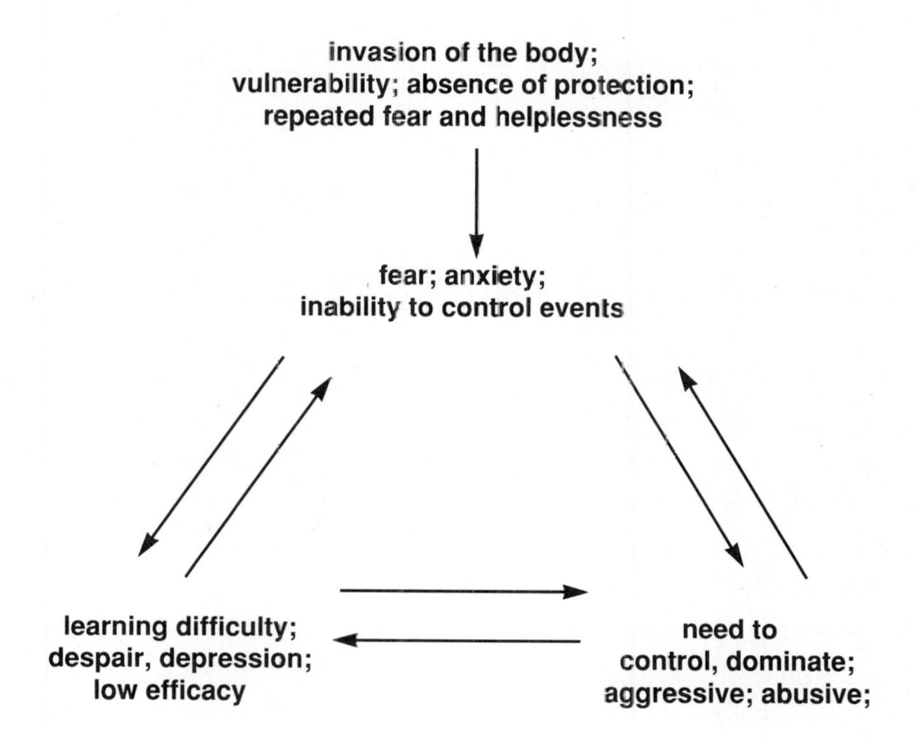

Powerlessness
invasion of the body;
vulnerability; absence of protection;
repeated fear and helplessness
fear; anxiety;
inability to control events
learning difficulty;
despair, depression;
low efficacy
need to
control, dominate;
aggressive; abusive;

tion, powerlessness and its response may well lead to the aggressive traumatising sexual acting out noted in children and young people who are abusing in response to their own abuse. Friedrich (1988) has pointed out the consistent description of differences between boys and girls who are abused. Girls are consistently described as showing an internalising response to abuse in terms of levels of anxiety, depression, low self-esteem, despair, phobic responses, whilst boys show a more characteristic externalising response. This would include the aggressive, dominating, abusive and sexualising pattern of behaviour. Some clinicians in talking about girls who abuse see them occasionally adopting an externalising mode (Fehrenbach and Monastersky, 1988), while some boys may adopt a far more internalising approach.

There are two further dynamics which add to traumatic sexualisation and powerlessness to assist the clinician in understanding the response of children and young people who are abusive.

Betrayal

Betrayal arises from the manipulation of the trust of the young person in an older person on whom he or she is dependent. Another factor is the violation of care which arises and the failure of protection and well-being created within positive family relationships. This may well lead, as in Figure 4, to a sense of depression, disenchantment and disillusion which interacts with a clinging dependent response seeking redeeming relationships. It is a characteristic of adolescents who have been abused to seek rapid replacement for relationships when there is any breakdown, for example, in girlfriend-boyfriend relating. There is often a clinging to quite unsuitable partners, and the creation of an illusion of needs being met, rather than having to face the feeling of aloneness, disenchantment and disillusion. Not surprisingly this pattern interacts with a sense of hostility and angry distrust in relationships and a tendency to retaliate and take an antisocial position.

Figure 4

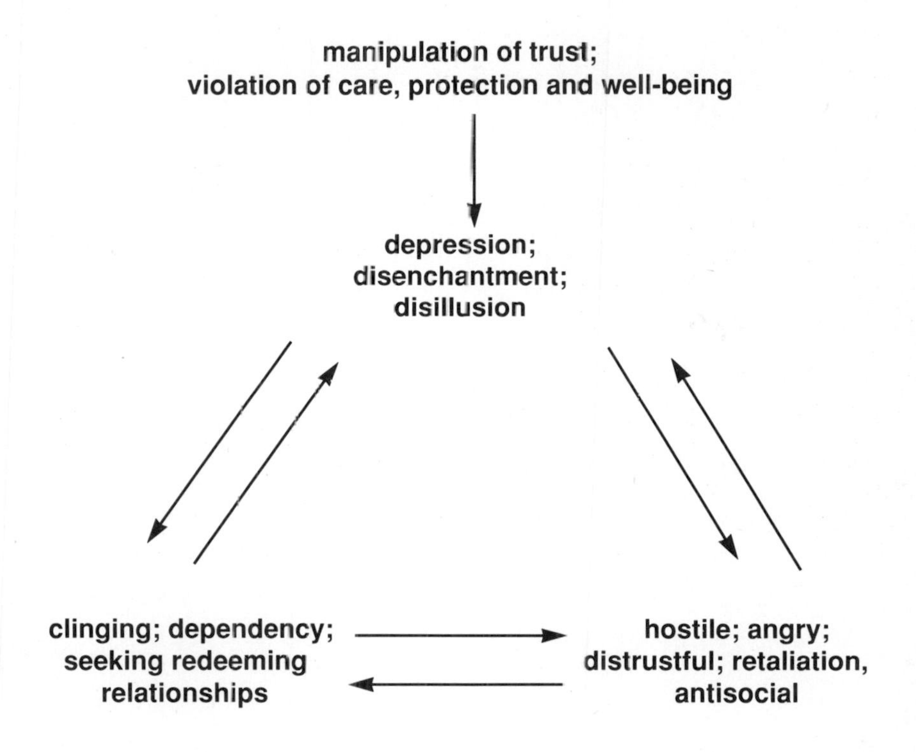
Betrayal
manipulation of trust;
violation of care, protection and well-being
depression;
disenchantment;
disillusion
clinging; dependency;
seeking redeeming
relationships
hostile; angry;
distrustful; retaliation,
antisocial

Stigmatisation

Stigmatisation arises from the tendency to blame the child or young person who is abused for any problems that arise, for example, needs for separation, blaming, self-blame for being the cause rather than being aware of the cognitive distortion set up within the abusive context.

Stigmatisation also arises out of the sense of secrecy, shame and embarrassment arising from being a sexual object. As some girls in a group stated 'We were used as prostitutes without being paid. They are paying the price to society by going to prison for a year, we are damaged forever'. The contempt which is so frequently a part of the use of the child or young person as a sexual object also adds to this sense. This can lead to a sense of isolation and marginalisation, perhaps taking on stigmatised roles, prostitution, drug use, promiscuity, or compulsive sexual activities of a powerful nature. These are all marginal roles within the peer group, and may well lead to the development of an aggressive style, to self or others.

A broader view of traumatic effects

Johnson's work indicates that girls who adopt abusive roles have almost all been abused. Research on boys who abuse, however indicates that perhaps around 50% have been abused sexually. It is therefore necessary to look beyond sexual abuse alone in the context of abuse as an explanatory model for those children and young people who do subsequently abuse.

Pierce and Pierce (1990) indicate that looking at the background of a series of adolescent offenders indicates a broad set of abusive experiences beyond sexual abuse. They describe a high incidence of physical abuse, emotional abuse and rejection, often associated with disruptions of care and a marginalisation of the young person within their family and peer group. It may be helpful to refer to work on the

Figure 5

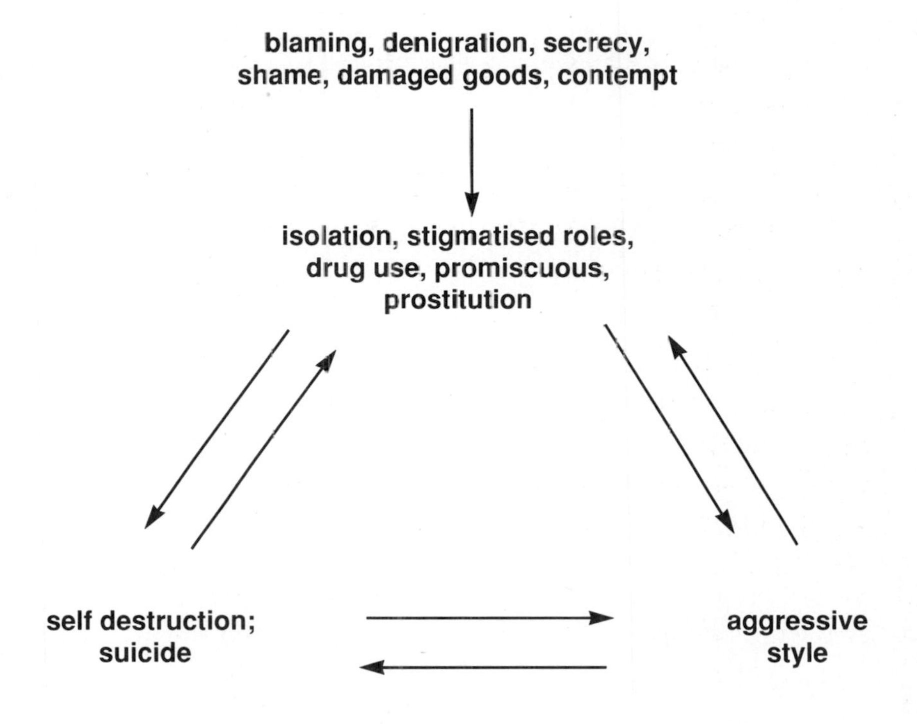
Stigmatisation
blaming, denigration, secrecy,
shame, damaged goods, contempt
isolation, stigmatised roles,
drug use, promiscuous,
prostitution
self destruction;
suicide
aggressive
style

development of a person's sense of self and the relationship to traumatic experiences (Cohen and Kinston, 1989, and Bentovim and Kinston, 1991). Psychoanalysts have been concerned with the way in which the development of the self occurs when abuse has occurred and self-protection is essential. It is noted that one response is the denial of the significance of the other. Deprivation of support and emotional nourishment leads to the development of a shell to ensure physical and psychic survival. Traumatic experiences within the family, traumatic handling of a child, can lead to a negative evaluation of the self since the inner core of the child is rejected or not recognised, while at the same time the shell ensures survival. Being treated as a 'thing' means others are treated as things; instead of attachment and care, there is use or abuse of the other and this pattern continues.

This results in a form of pseudo-relating, for example, the clinging, dependent, response seeking, redeeming relationships of the betrayed child, the victim roles of the stigmatised child. Alternatively there may be an apparent failure to relate. Hostile, angry, isolated, responses occur with an absence of any form of empathy, caring or warmth. There may be a third alternative: a need-driven, poor ability to relate, with aggressive, retaliatory, distrustful, abusive-manipulative responses to the other. Such response to trauma in a very broad sense occurs beyond sexual abuse, and may occur as a response to a variety of traumatic handling of children.

Becker (1988) has proposed a broad contextual model, to encompass sexually abusive adolescents, within the frame of the individual, family and society. She notes that within the individual context issues such as social isolation, conduct disorder, limited cognitive abilities, impulsive disorders (Kavoussi *et al*, 1988), and a history of physical or sexual abuse may well lead to the abusive patterns described above. Within the family context when parents are engaging in coercive sexual or physical behaviours towards each other, or have a belief system supportive of coercive sexual behaviours this contributes to a modelling effect. Poor interpersonal skills and lack of empathy also provide a major contribution. Society's support of coercive sexual behaviours, sexualisation of children and peergroup pressures also trigger antisocial behaviour and may well also be a major contribution to such behavioural patterns.

Glasgow (1990) also includes factors such as the inconsistency of values and attitudes in adolescence, the intensity and variability of effect such as adolescent turmoil, the intensity of libido during adolescence, and the difficulty of appraising and relating internal events to external behaviour. He also notes the absence of well established patterns of sexual relationships, and apparently spontaneous sexual arousal events, and the non-sexual sensation seeking patterns in delinquent adolescents which may well trigger abusive acts. Having an egocentric approach with a low degree of social altruism may also have an effect in reducing empathy and concerns.

Finkelhor's four-factor model to understand the triggering of abuse (Finkelhor, 1984) also contributes. This relates factors such as early abuse which creates the sexual interest in children, and factors which overcome internal and external inhibitions to action. Adolescence itself, the proximity of siblings, and particularly children brought together from different families in reconstituted family situations may well enable young people to cross the boundaries of sexualised behaviour. Younger children are, by definition, far more vulnerable and more easily silenced by siblings and young people who have a good deal of contact with them.

All these factors basically link to the notion that if during development a child is treated as a thing instead of a person, then he or she will treat the other as a thing. Where there is an absence or a loss of caring responses, sexually aggressive impulses of early childhood and later adolescence have full rein, particularly when such feelings are associated with a long-standing sense of grievance through poor care and disruption during development.

Specific mechanisms leading to abusive behaviour in boys and girls

It is possible to summarise the psychogenic dynamics described earlier by indicating that:

- there is an extensive sexualisation of intra and inter-personal experiences;
- a sexualisation of subordination arises.

This confusion of sexuality leads to the emotional and cognitive effects of stigmatisation, powerlessness and betrayal and to a negative evaluation of their own victimisation. Therefore considerable confusion exists about appropriate and inappropriate actions and responses to stress and anxiety. When children have grown up in intense role reversal with their mothers, for instance, the illusion of adult active roles is created for boys and girls. When this is associated with family models of physical aggression and coercive parental styles, it can lead to intense acting out through sexual pathways.

Being forced to participate in sibling abuse, and mothers participating in abuse is another factor leading to sexually abusing acting out, and Johnson (1989) has noted that girls in particular abuse other children who are perceived as favoured as a way of sharing such experiences in a retaliatory way. Re-enactment of abuse in a broad way leads to temporary relief, but in turn simulates the cycle with little pleasure.

One of the very real issues which needs to be considered is the differences in sexual activities between children who abuse and adolescents who abuse. Friedrich (1988) has pointed out the thinking differences between children and adolescents in terms of concrete thinking of children and the more abstract abilities of older children and young people. When young children are abused the experiences are integrated with and part of their early cognitive and emotional views of the world. Adolescents who are abused for the first time see experiences as quite separate from earlier ways of understanding themselves and their relationships. Indeed, it is a common phenomenon to note that young children who have been abused for many years may well only come to perceive the abnormality of their experiences when they reach adolescence.

To illustrate the mechanisms two cases will be described:

Katy C

Katy was 10 when she was referred to us. She was referred by a social services department because it had become clear some months previously that she was extensively involved in sexual activities with other children. After having been removed from her own family because of extensive abuse and neglect, she had been placed in a variety of different contexts finally being placed for adoption. This had broken down and at the time of referral she was placed with experienced professional foster parents. After her sexual activities had been noted, investigation revealed that she had been involved with sexual activities and sexually abusive incidents with approximately 29 children within her own first family, various foster placements and her current foster home. The following patterns were revealed.

In her own family she had three half brothers with whom she described playing mums and dads; Katy as mum and one of the half brothers as dad. She described that they had 'actual sex' together, both being naked, the brother lying on top and Katy moving up and down. She described mutual oral sex, open-mouthed kissing using the tongue, digital penetration of each other's anus and Katy's vagina. The other half brothers would pretend to be offspring and Katy would stimulate all the boys' penises and digitally penetrate their anuses and would use various objects including combs which she rubbed their penises with. She also described being forced to watch her mother and stepfather's sexual activities. She described being taught to kiss open-mouthed using her tongue by her stepfather and mother, and to masturbate men and women by watching her parents masturbate each other and being masturbated herself by them. She described being participant with her mother and stepfather, digital penetration and masturbation, vaginal intercourse and oral sex.

When placed with various foster parents after being removed from her home at five years she described similar patterns with the children of foster parents and neighbours' children. She talked about pretending to have sex with the boys, showing boys how to masturbate her for instance. She described touching the vagina of baby foster children because she wanted to feel what it was like. She also described being asked to dress an 18-year-old mentally handicapped child and fondling and kissing her breasts and nipples, also taking her to the toilet, wiping her vagina and stroking her anus and digitally penetrating her. Some of the children who she involved in the same pattern of behaviour responded while others refused to participate, even pushed her off vigorously. A two-year-old boy tried to bite her or push her hand away when she attempted to penetrate his anus digitally.

Neighbouring children of, for example, nine and 10 years of age, may have repulsed her attempts to get them to reciprocate vaginal and anal penetration, told her to get off, keep her hands to herself, but Katy persisted in her attempts. She described becoming so excited at times that she wet the bed, talked about feeling nice, excited, her vagina feeling all tingly and wet, and enjoying seeing neighbouring children naked. She talked about feeling particularly excited because the 18-

year-old was an adult. She described a mutual contact with a boy at school and there was some confusion whether Katy was taking the active role or whether the boy was more active than she was. There was clearly an issue about whether this boy had also been abused.

With children she met in other placements she would pretend that, for instance, a five-year-old was her baby and attempted to feed her at her breast, and at the same time penetrating, stimulating and the child refusing to reciprocate. At times she was discovered, for instance, in a red faced state on top of other children. She is also described as being flirtatious with an adolescent boy and his friends, and described having fantasies about being with such young men. She masturbated intensively, but increasingly in a private way so it was as if she had become clever at not being spotted. At interview she described her sense of retaliation and revenge, her desire, as it were to 'get rid of' her own feelings of arousal and intense feelings and fantasies, and also something of the excitement and arousal experienced.

Katy is an example of a girl who had been abused extensively before the age of five, showing her continuing pattern. As she approached the pre-pubertal period of development, she was now taking on a far more adolescent approach to sexual activities, for example, her fantasies in relationship to older adolescent boys, her description of her genital arousal in relationship to specifically sexual activities. Johnson (1989) has indicated that younger children who are involved in abusive activities describe a more diffuse sense of tension, relieved by sexual activities without the specific sexual focus and fantasies described by this girl as she moved towards puberty. The therapeutic task is to help her regain her childhood.

Paul

Another case which demonstrates the way in which a set of fantasies can be created for the adolescent boy of a perverse nature is demonstrated in the case of Paul who was seen at the age of 14. He too had been placed with foster parents following a long history of abuse, neglect and a coercive family context. Concern arose because he was beginning to become involved in abusive acts with younger foster children and their friends.

Paul could only describe one stable period in his life before his parents took up a nomadic existence.

His father died when he was 10, and his mother described an unhappy childhood herself despite having a wealthy context to grow up in. Her teenage years were spent in isolation with increasing flights into a fantasy world, and there were periods of irrational outbursts and violent attacks on her parents. She was also epileptic and difficult to cope with. She had disappeared from home for ten years, changed her name and married and had Paul. There was concern about Paul's development, he was noted to be lacking in stimulation, was neglected, poorly fed, distressed in school. After his father's death when he was 12, it was noted that he committed a stealing offence with another boy, who his mother was sheltering. The home was filthy, his mother was in a strange mental state and it was noted that he had an odd relationship with his mother.

Paul continued to offend with an older boy of 17 living in his mother's flat. At the age of 13, he was removed from home. He had been poorly cared for and he revealed that both he and his mother had been assaulted physically by the young man living there. He revealed at a later date that he had been buggered by the young man, involved in masturbation, oral sex and other sex games and forced to take part in oral, anal and vaginal sex with his mother. Bestiality was also involved and Paul revealed major concerns about his own identity and orientation.

When seen, he had been separated from his mother for 18 months and was beginning to be aware of a sense of outrage and a deeply held sense of grievance. He also admitted with considerable difficulty that he enjoyed some of the sexual contact he had experienced and was missing it. He took part in a group (to be described later) and the structure of his fantasy and cognitive attitudes revealed the basis of the shift from being abused to taking on abusive attitudes.

On a number of questionnaires listed by Salter (Salter, 1988) he revealed his pattern. To the Wilson Sexual Fantasy Questionnaire (Wilson, 1978) he answered positively to the following: having sex with someone much younger than yourself and having sex with someone much older than yourself; tying someone up and being tied up; and seducing an innocent. He also responded positively to questions about being excited by material or clothing, and using objects for stimulation. To the Abel and Becker Cognition Scales (Abel *et al*, 1989) he agreed to the following statements: that a man (or woman) is justified with having sex with his (or her) children or step-children, if his wife (husband) does not like sex; a child who doesn't physically resist an adult's sexual advances really wants to have sex with the adult; an adult just feeling a child's body all over without touching her (his) genitals is not really being sexual with a child; if an adult has sex with a younger child it prevents the child having sexual hang-ups in the future; and there is no effective treatment for child molestation. He also marked many items positively on the Buss/Durkee Hostility Inventory (Buss and Durkee, 1957).

The notion of the abusive cycle

The observations in these two clinical cases, together with many others, suggest that the notion of the sexually abusive cycle which has been described in adults also applies to adolescent perpetrators and presumably also links to children.

Earlier the trauma cycle was described, linking abusive acts to overwhelming feelings of anxiety, deletion phenomena and then re-enactment action in place of feelings which could not be dealt with or worked through. This becomes incorporated into a perpetrator cycle, as patterns of activities are enacted, and become self-fulfilling, through the addictive nature of sexualisation or arousal patterns.

Ryan *et al* (1987) have described two dysfunctional cycles, one of which is involved with cognitive distortions and activities, the other cycle being the assault cycle itself. Figure 6 is the perpetrator's cycle described by adolescents in the group conducted by Cardoza and Hamblian (1990). A cycle of this nature needs to be made far more complex in the way that Ryan *et al* have described; so start at the point of sexual touching which leads to erection, add to this anger and/or power behaviour, and deal with this by externalising blame on the victim rather than feeling responsible. This leads to feelings of guilt, hopes that the victim won't be there again, and perhaps a determination that the young person won't abuse again associated with a sense of poor self image and self-esteem. Then the compulsion to think about activities reoccurs, with a division of feelings, wanting to stop, but knowing that it is not possible to stop.

Feelings of arousal increase as masturbation occurs, including to the particular victim-child of a particular age. This strengthens the cognitive set, together with the sense of grievance and frustration associated with poor care and relationship difficulties. This may well lead to touching in a non-sexual way, erection and then assaultative behaviour. There may well also be planning, rehearsal, victim selection and grooming in the process of choosing the particular victim as part of the cycle. There may well be a complex set of fantasies, feelings and desires within the arousal masturbatory pattern. Ryan *et al* (1987) describe young people's fantasies as attempting to resolve rejections and grievances through omnipotent fantasies involving movie stars or

Figure 6

Adolescent perpetrators' cycle

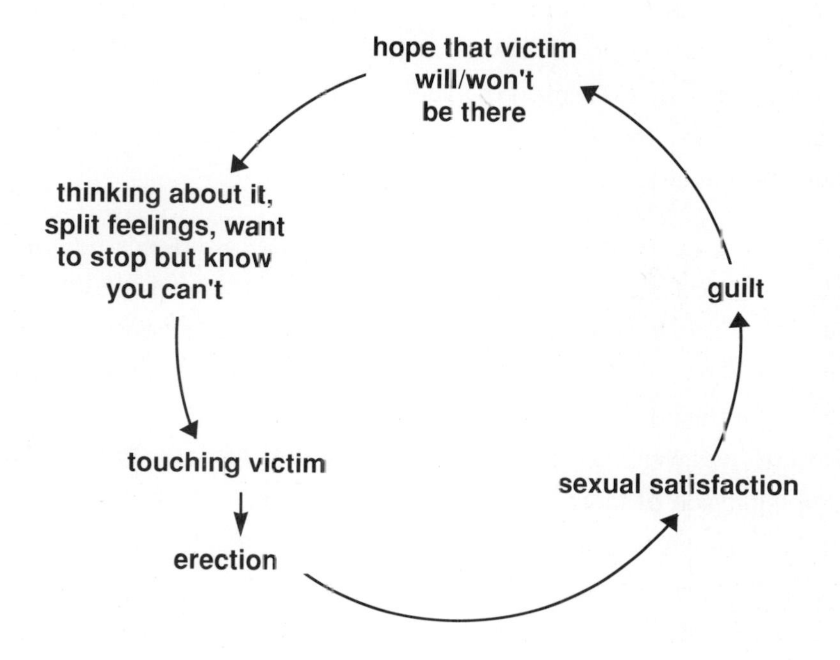

a teacher. Negative feelings may be evoked including overpowering, defiling and degrading feelings towards the victim in the way that Paul responded to the questionnaires – true identification with the aggressor.

Profiling perpetrator patterns

One of the major concerns in looking at the different perpetrator cycles is the necessity of differentiating different abusive behaviours. Ryan (1986) carried out a literature review on adolescent perpetrators of sexual molestation of children, and various studies are referred to, comparing non-sexually assaultative boys with sexually assaultative males, particularly those prone to violent aggressive sexual attacks. There is a stress in the literature on not underplaying the issue of adolescent and children's experimentation, since such patterns may well be associated with the sort of cycle of behaviour over time described above.

This was revealed in a 16-year-old boy, Carl, who was referred from a special school because of his sexual abusive behaviour with other children. He was functioning at about a 13–14 year level, and he grew up in a family with grandparents. His grandmother was a prostitute who entertained clients, and he was made to watch, to enact sex with siblings, and with the grandmother. He described his feelings of anger and confusion at times when he for instance touched the breasts of another girl in the school. By the device of talking about 'another Carl', rather than himself, he was able to reveal his intense arousal towards female members of staff. He talked about powerful compulsions to touch their breasts, and also revealed an extensive rape scenario which he had developed in his mind associated with intense feelings of confusion.

He found it very difficult indeed to know where to put responsibility for his feelings. Was his arousal to adult females' breasts their responsibility or his? He was aware that his grandmother had undressed in front of him and he was not sure therefore whether his arousal was her responsibility or his. His sense of confusion associated with the arousal linking with the traumagenic dynamics described previously, evoked an aggressive-abusive role out of identification with his own experiences of being treated as a thing. Therefore, he felt it was appropriate to treat the other as a thing.

It was felt that this young man, with his ability to split himself into caring and non-caring selves, was seriously at risk of carrying out abusive acts. He was attributing arousal to the other's intention to make him excited, rather than being aware that he was in contact with his own abusive experiences, through flashbacks and cognitive distortions of his own experiences. One of the major problems for staff was to know how to help him deal with his feeling of arousal. If he was encouraged to masturbate using the masturbatory satiation technique (Abel *et al*, 1987) to, for instance, a soft pornographic magazine as a more normative stimulus, would this not reinforce his feelings about a woman revealing herself to him as invitation?

Devising appropriate scenarios to help young people develop more normative sexual orientations is clearly problematic, and with young children it is extremely difficult to sort out what are the appropriate ways of helping a child recover normative infantile sexuality, rather than the enforced adult pattern.

Treatment approaches for adolescent perpetrators

Ryan in her summary of the literature (Ryan, 1986) describes the agreement which existed amongst practitioners at the point of her reviews for adolescent perpetrators. In the USA in 1987, 470 programmes and service providers were available to adolescent offenders (Knopp 1982). In the UK we are much earlier in the development of such programmes and an early offenders group for adolescent perpetrators will be described. Ryan's consensus statement for those working with adolescent offenders encompasses the following:

- Adolescent sex offenders must be held accountable for their inappropriate sexual acts.
- They must receive 'sex offence specific' treatment, that is rather than treatment focusing on some general aspect of meeting their needs in terms of appropriate care.
- The treatment mode of choice is a peer group setting with individual, behavioural and family treatment as an adjunct.
- Certain risk assessment criteria can help determine the relative safety of choosing an out patient approach in the community, or whether there is a need for residential placement.

  This is a major issue since the trend within the general field of delinquency and management of adolescence is towards community treatment with the phasing out of many residential settings. Yet at the same time it is becoming clear that although professional fostering, and community resources are currently the trend, there is strong evidence of a group of young people who require residential settings to contain them and to provide the intensity of therapeutic work. There is clearly a need for therapeutic communities which can meet the needs of such children. Glasgow (1990) has commented on the advantages of dispersal of children with residential needs amongst a number of settings rather than the focusing of such children within one institution in terms of having abused sexually.

Decisions about residential care versus remaining within the community and foster families, or their own families, are clearly linked to the degree of risk to children either within their own particular home, or within the community. Young people whose abusive behaviour includes violence, or involves large numbers of children, clearly have very different needs from those who have abused one or two children and do not use coercion in their contact. It also requires examination of the abusive cycle described earlier (see Figure 6).

- Treatment of the young person should cover identifiable areas and the programme followed will be described in detail. Not only does the issue of the abusive pattern need to be considered and how to reverse and create more benign patterns, but also other issues to do with normative data on sexual development and contraception. Social skills, anger, control and diversion development of empathy, dealing with their own abuse and victimisation are also important areas.

- Court involvement is an asset facilitating engagement and following through in treatment. Probation Orders can facilitate long term work, as can the involvement of social services and use of appropriate care proceedings when necessary. This is an important difference between the trend in dealing with juvenile delinquency. Currently there is a move towards the use of diversion rather than court involvement in management of delinquency. Delinquency has been described as a normative phase for many young people and the concept of growing out of crime, rather than being involved in the criminal justice system and therefore learning more about crime, appears to be an appropriate way of dealing with many delinquents. Intermediate treatment and community service within the community itself is seen as a helpful approach with the use of formal warnings.

We need to take seriously the long term early experiences of adults who have commenced their abusive action during adolescence, and the increasing number of young people who are abusing younger children significantly. We have to be concerned about long term effects, and therefore the possibility of being able to follow up young people for a reasonable period of time following the awareness of their abuse.

Glasgow (1990) has pointed out the considerable difficulties in making alliances with young people who abuse, and the considerable difficulties in finding out what is happening to their abusive patterns. He feels that the use of appropriate legal processes, probation and prosecution, offers a window of opportunity to make a link with the young person and this might ensure that over time there is some hope of finding out what is happening to the young person in terms of his or her behaviour. Smith and Monastersky (1986) and Hengler (1989) indicate the variability of re-offending in young people (between 14% and 44% after between two-and-a-half and three years) which raises concerns if there is not a close monitoring of the young person.

It is possible for a young person to be convicted of rape as early as 14 years, and there has been discussion as to whether the charge should be available for younger children. In fact it is perfectly possible with younger children to use Care Proceedings to maintain a link with such a young person. Experiences with treatment of sexual abuse in general would indicate that a combination of an appropriate response to a criminal act, for example, Probation Order with some appropriate treatment, together with a Care Order where the appropriate care placement can be considered is often a helpful combination. There are of course many controversies about the issue of the role of criminal proceedings, probation officers working with younger offenders, and the role of social service departments, as well as psychiatric provisions which are very limited for adolescents as specific treatment contexts.

Ryan (1986) comments that although clinicians working with adult offenders are somewhat pessimistic about their ability to bring about long term change, clinicians working with juvenile offenders are guardedly optimistic that by confronting the problem during the formative years of adolescence, some lasting changes may be possible. She comments that 'a multi-disciplinary approach, wherein law enforcement, the courts, clinicians and communities work together, promises to have a significant impact on stemming the development of a new generation of sex offenders'.

Treatment approaches for young children

The SPARK programme (Support Programme for Abuse Reactive Kids) was developed for children under the age of 13 by Kee MacFarlane, and implemented in 1985 (Johnson and Berry, 1989). This was the first programme specifically aimed at young children.

As far as the treatment programme for young children is concerned, Johnson and Berry (1989) advocate the use of a peer group; a group setting, with parallel work available for parents or caretakers as well as the abused or non abused siblings. Thus in both the adolescent and children's field, there is a move towards an approach which capitalises on the effect of working together with peers in a group context. This can in turn be linked to group work with other family members, alongside family and appropriate individual work to create a systemic framework of treatment related to the management of trauma and traumatic effects. Similar approaches have been described for abused children and their families generally (Bentovim *et al*, 1988).

Special issues in the management of sexual abuse of children and young people

Bentovim *et al* (1988) described the stages of management of sexual abuse in general as occurring in four stages:

- the disclosure stage;
- stage of separation of the abuser from the abused children;
- rehabilitation to family contexts;
- placement in new family contexts.

Disclosure stage

It is already clear from the description of the context in which children abuse that those abusing most severely are often living in a disruptive setting where there may be poor care and other forms of abuse. There are often major problems in helping children and young people take appropriate responsibility for abuse which is reported against them. This may well be supported by the family who may minimise, disbelieve the child who is making a complaint, and support their older child against the child making the allegation.

The complexity for a child who has been severely abused who then becomes an abuser is mirrored by the complexity for the parent who has one child as victim and the other as abuser. The complexity of emotional alliances for parents causes enormous stress. There are problems enough when a non-abusive parent has to balance her emotions between her partner who has abused and her child who has been abused in terms of her own needs and her responsibilities. It is even harder for the parent who has to balance between children, where one has been abused and the other is the abuser, or in relationship to their own children, who may have abused against other children, or may have been abused as well as abusing.

The complexity increases when there needs to be an investigation as to whether the older child who abuses has also been abused. It seems almost certain that 100% of girls who abuse have been abused, and about half of boys who abuse have been abused. Both girls and boys may also have experienced a variety of other privations and abusive experiences at the same time as their abuse or earlier. There has been a tendency for the lead in investigating the abusing child to be taken by the police. This may well result in limited horizons to the investigation, losing both the complexity and range of information which might be revealed if other professionals were involved in such an investigation. One view may be that if a child is abusing, he or she requires the same joint investigation by police and social workers as the child who has been abused. There would need to be a similar programme including strategy meetings and networking of information about the child to assess whether detailed investigation of other family members and family context are required. All this information could then be brought together at a case conference before decisions were made about how best to progress.

Given the number of tasks that have to be considered and the issues, time is often needed to make a measured assessment of the situation. While this may be possible when dealing with the abused child, there is more pressure on time when dealing with the abusing child. There may well be a need for an immediate residential placement for the young person while the offences are investigated. There needs to be a full exploration in a multi-level way of the individual who has abused, consideration of his or her own abuse and consideration of whether other children in his context have been abused or are abusing. Additionally the family's attitudes and capacities for protection of other children or the child who has abused must be assessed so that longer term decisions can be shared between agencies and disciplines about where he or she needs to live in the longer term. Such decisions may well depend on the assessment of attitudes such as whether the abusive child or young person is blamed, is victimised him or herself and the degrees of family confusion and rejection that are present. It is also very important to assess any other children living within the family: they may well also be at risk if the young person has abused externally, or they may have been abused already. Again it is necessary to assess whether the parents are taking an appropriately serious attitude to the offence rather than minimising it, or to explore if they are hostile towards care and investigation authorities. Where the family has an attitude of bitterness, recrimination and hostility to authority, the likelihood of an inappropriate protective response and minimising the actions of the child who has abused may be noted. Alternatively the young person may be excluded and blamed, and may require care for his or her own protection. Thus it is only out of consideration of all these issues that decisions can be made about where the child is living, whether care or criminal processes are appropriate, and where the child needs to live short term and perhaps longer term.

It is also essential to assess what work the family is able to engage in, and to examine areas of family dysfunction which may have contributed to or facilitated a young person's abusive behaviour. Also it is necessary to assess family communication, boundary, maintenance, parenting capacities, and the general sense of competence and collaboration with the community. Such information often needs to be set before an appropriate court, whether in civil child care, or in criminal proceedings. A coordinated multidisciplinary, multi-agency response is as essential for the child who abuses as for the child who is abused. In many cases they are one and the same child.

Stage of separation

Separation may be effected through the young person living in a residential setting, a therapeutic community context, or a specialised foster family. Separation implies either separation from the child of the family who has been abused by the older child, or from other children whom he or she may be liable to abuse. Ryan (1986) advocated groupwork approaches assisted by behavioural and family work. It is essential that victims also be given appropriate treatment, and group and family treatment being available for parents and siblings.

A group for parents who have children that have been abused and children who are abusing is helpful in terms of sharing some of the stressful and extremely painful issues. Parents often feel torn apart by the separate needs of victim and perpetrator, and their ambivalence and intense mixture of feelings needs a good deal of help in sharing and coming to terms with. Parents need a similar programme to children, both in terms of learning what areas their children are dealing with, but also in thinking of different aspects of their own parenting issues.

Helpful themes for such groups are behaviour which had been observed before disclosure of abuse; understanding the nature of traumatic patterns, abusive and victim behaviour; managing behavioural difficulties; linking their own experiences of stress and abuse to their children's responses; integrating the needs of their children who had been abused and who were abusing; being able to work cooperatively with professionals in these areas.

The necessity for older children to be able to apologise to younger children is an important aspect of the phase of separation. In the phase of disclosure it is often helpful if there can be some acknowledgement from the older child that he or she is responsible, not the younger child. At a later stage it is often possible for the young person to go more deeply into his feelings of penitence and sadness for the child who has been victimised and to make a more formal and perhaps more deeply felt apology. Madanes (1989) has described a programme where she gets an older young person who has abused literally to go on his knees to the child who has been abused within the family context, and other family members similarly to beg forgiveness from the child, both for the abuse and for the failure to note and protect. Bentovim and Ratner (1991) described the intense emotional atmosphere which can accompany an apology session at the appropriate time within the overall therapeutic process.

Rehabilitation phase

This phase indicates that work has been completed with the abuser whether of a child in his/her own family or in the community. Family members need to have completed the task of understanding the origin of the young person's abusive behaviour, and their own roles.

They need to participate in joint family work on issues which still remain, working collaboratively with professionals who are needing to continue assessing the child.

The view expressed by Bentovim *et al* (1988) on the relationship between group and individual treatment is that once there has been the opportunity of working with the generic issues of group work, it is helpful to consider the individual needs of children and young people following the completion of a programme. Masturbatory satiation techniques, and covert sensitisation techniques described by Abel *et al* (1987) are behavioural approaches dealing with abusive fantasies. They teach techniques of masturbating to normative sexual fantasies, and then attempting to masturbate to deviant fantasies immediately following, or to introduce negative punitive outcomes. They require individual work with young people rather than work in a group context. Many individual and family issues need to be picked up with the child, young person and his specific family, rather than being dealt with in a group context. Social skills, development of empathic responses which are part of general group work, need to be extended to developmental work in residential settings and therapeutic communities, as well as foster homes and through family work. Individual dynamically orientated psychotherapy also has a place in dealing with remaining deviancy and interpersonal problems.

New family placements

There will always be a number of children, as in the general approach to child abuse, who require new family placements. This may be because of rejection by their families, or such dysfunctional problems within the family that the changes necessary to protect, contain or adequately supervise the child cannot be made. It may therefore be that the short term foster placements become longer term, or are necessary when rejection or failure to integrate in their own families becomes a reality. There is clearly room for extensive surveys of abusing children and young people in the UK, to look at the patterns of what happens to them and what are the responses to the various approaches which are attempted in various parts of the country.

A group work programme for young people

Cardoza and Hamblian (1990) developed a group work approach for young people referred to the Sexual Abuse Treatment Programme of the Hospital for Sick Children, Great Ormond Street. This was an unselected group from the young people referred to the programme by referral agents from around the London area and beyond to the Home Counties. There is a tendency to refer young people who are more seriously abused or abusing to a tertiary centre, and this was the case amongst the young people referred and treated.

A decision was made to select out alcohol/substance abuse and violent histories but in fact none of the young people referred had such a problem. There was one 17-year-old and the rest gathered around the 13, 14, 15 range. It was felt that it would be helpful for there to be an admission of perpetration of abuse, but it was decided that this was not as important as an agreement to attend which it was felt was essential. It was decided not to coerce the young people to attend, but there were preliminary meetings where it was made clear that if somebody was abusing at their age, then there was a real problem of becoming a sex offender, and this possibility had to be faced. One of the young people who had been abused was alleged to have abused extensively. Although initially he did not accept responsibility for his abusive actions, he was prepared to attend because of the 'alleged' offences he had committed. After a number of sessions he was able to take responsibility for his abuse saying that if others could he could.

It was decided that Statutory Orders were not essential as legal responses were so variable in this group, and if there had been a limitation to prosecution cases it would have limited the group to children aged 15+. Some children were in care already and others were motivated by parental concerns and always linked with agencies concerned with abuse in any case. Profiling of the young people was carried out before the group started, based on Wyre's pack on treatment of sexual abuse (Wyre, 1989).

There was extensive use of questionnaires, paper and pencil tests, since they seemed an excellent way to engage young people in work tasks rather than attempting discussion topics alone. Our experience with young children and with boys' groups previously was that unless there are specific tasks which engage children and young people, restlessness and defensive behaviour takes over. The group leaders were a man and woman with considerable experience of working with young people. They found containing and managing the group more stressful towards the end of groups, but generally did not feel they were uncontained. The theme of needing to avoid becoming an offender was a powerful one which was maintained in the front of people's minds and this had an impact on them through the life of the group.

A good deal of the material available for groups is focused on adults, for example, the set of questionnaires in Salter (1988). However, so many of these severely abused children had been involved in sado-masochistic abuse, bestiality, oral sex and violence in their own victim experiences, that the content of questionnaires focused on adult abusers was not outside their experiences.

Themes and approaches

Although a number of the young people referred were victims, it was decided that it was important to deal with perpetration patterns first, so that young people could be confronted with the fact that they could not use their own victimisation as an excuse. It was important to establish sexual language immediately and to decide on a non-sexist appropriate language which would be kept to within the group. The young people were taken seriously and they would be treated and expected to treat the leaders with respect. It was important for workers to support each other, appreciate gender issues and give group members hope, information and space.

Topics and sessions

The first group that was carried out lasted over twelve sessions. To some extent it was felt that twelve was the maximum that children of this age could tolerate, but the approach followed appeared to contain young people and it was felt that it would be preferable to extend the sessions to approximately sixteen. The sessions lasted for one and a quarter hours, and it was extremely important to ensure that the group members were normally accompanied to sessions by carers, residential workers, or their social workers to ensure attendance, and also that the stressful responses to dealing with some of the issues could be picked up within the group context. Parent groups were available for those parents who were attending, and a Caretaking group was available for residential workers or foster parents accompanying young people.

Session plans

This incorporates both what was delivered and some suggestions for a programme. The detailed content will be published in due course.

- Session one

Introductions, establishing rules, hopes and fears for the group, development of sexual language using body maps to chart these.

Developing an agreed language for the group.

- Session two

A group exercise ranking sexual acts, using cards stating as many of the different sexual acts, appropriate and inappropriate, that members and leaders could list. This is an exercise which can bring in discussion and an ease of talking about sexually inappropriate acts, and voicing their language. It acts to reduce the intense degree of anxiety surrounding their own acts, fantasies and experiences, and begins to initiate the process of being able to process this material cognitively.

- Session three – Normal dating cycle

A decision was made about looking at normal dating cycle before offending cycles which proved helpful. This was again a group exercise trying to list the steps in making normal relationships or the normal cycle of meeting the opposite sex. The group devised the steps, 28 in all, towards making a sexual contact in a normal appropriate consensual way. For instance part of the pattern was trying to be in the same place at the same time as somebody to whom one was attracted, speaking with her even if only teasing or joking, fantasies developing, possibly masturbation, possibly asking for a date in a group preferably, then eventually going out together and trying for non sexual touches, being aware of the other's response, and of finding appropriate ways of being given permission and seeking consent at all times.

- Sessions four to seven – Cycles of offending

This is perhaps the central and most important period of group work. It involves getting each boy to work out his specific cycle of offending in considerable detail and checking this out with each other. It was found that it was helpful to leave discussion of this until this point in the group's life since group members were far more confident in each other by this time. They were also more articulate, having found the appropriate language to describe their cycles.

- Sessions seven to nine – Victims' responses

These sessions examined exactly what they did to their victims, using victim statements, and again sought a list of responses from group members. Lists produced included feelings such as worthlessness, only being valuable for sex; bodies reacting sexually although he or she may hate what is happening; worries about homosexuality with the same-sex abuser; having flash-backs at uncontrolled times; remembering the assault; confused; mixed up; worried about damage to sex organs; worries about having children in the future; worries about assaulting others; anger, fear and no trust.

- Session ten

Personal issues raised by the group, inside and outside the group.

- Session eleven

Showing videos available following public television programmes about male perpetrators, and beginning the process of linking their perpetration with their victimisation.

- Session twelve – Sex education

- Session thirteen – Contraception

- Session fourteen

Strategies to prevent re-offending and what happens if people offend again.
Introducing some of the principles of blocking and cognitive structuring towards more appropriate fantasies and masturbating.

- Session fifteen

Further sessions on strategies to prevent re-offending.

- Session sixteen

Celebration and advice for the future

Although a number of similar group programmes have been described, in particular by Glasgow (1990), they are programmes which attempt to deal with the broad aspects of the problems and some may be limited in their applicability. There is a significant absence of controlled trials of treatment approaches: the ethical dilemmas of withholding treatment, giving treatment or not, are considerable. It is hoped that the sort of approach described above meets the three areas delineated by Wheeler and Berliner (1988) as important in:

- dealing with anxiety arousal;
- dealing with cognitive distortions;
- dealing with major sexual behavioural and attitude problems.

Working with children in the pre-adolescent period is far less well explored. Johnson and Berry (1989) state that 'Whilst intrapsychic pain and confusion must be attended to, these children have chosen to act out this pain in an interpersonal manner. To treat the problem, its interpersonal aspects must be addressed directly, and in the context of persons interacting together. It is not our aim to have the child perpetrator to be able to interact one to one with an adult, but to be able to be with other children without being sexually inappropriate with them. In the group we talk about sexual issues which often stimulate the children. From this they can learn how to identify these feelings and prevent themselves from acting on them. Skills which are needed include problem solving; social skills; impulse control; perspective taking; identification; and expression of a wide range of feelings; anger management; cognitive strategies for controlling behaviour; and task completion for mastery. Themes to be explored include trust, betrayal, secrecy, guilt, loss of self esteem, power/powerlessness, confusion, fear, body image, victimisation, perpetration, responsibility, blame, leader versus follower, assertion/aggression, sexual feelings, sibling rivalry, substance abuse, cognitive distortions and behaviour patterns'.

The groups followed some well worn paths, sharing of snacks, talking about good and not so good things, and structured activities, skills and themes being integrated. Role-plays, dramatic enactment, and games were introduced. Perpetrators were grouped according to gender and age, 5–7, 8–10 and 11–13. Groups are extensive and may well continue for two or three terms in parallel with Parents and Sibling groups.

Conclusion

In the UK concern about young people and children who are abusing is growing. We have been aware for some years about the problem of adolescent perpetrators, but the tendency has been for them to be seen as a sub-group of a violently delinquent population rather than a particular group in their own right. Concern has arisen initially through our awareness of the extensive long term effects of abuse on children. We have become increasingly aware of the nature of the abusive act in terms of the perpetrator, we have also known for some time that a good deal of abuse is perpetrated within the generation of childhood rather than across generations but we are now being forced to act on this information.

Until now the focus has been on the major trauma of abuse as experienced in relationship to somebody significantly older, particularly a parent figure, and his child victim. We are now concerned with other abusers, with women, with young people – and now children as abusers. Work with children and young people as abusers needs to be integrated into the total concern for abused children since so many have been both subject to abuse and are re-enacting their own abuse. This may have been sexual abuse, or it may have been other forms of traumatic handling which have led to re-enactment in a sexual context. Inevitably this feeds back into a general concern about sexuality in the community, what children know, what they learn, what education they have both in terms of knowledge and protection. This in turn leads to societal attitudes, and the implicit and explicit messages we give about sexuality in the community, which may have a part in providing models for traumatic and traumatising patterns of behaviour.

Issues for the way ahead

■

DR EILEEN VIZARD

These comments are intended to provide a brief review of key issues which have emerged during the last decade in the field of working with child sexual abuse in the United Kingdom. This review is intended to offer guidance on how we may begin to meet the new challenges of work in this field. Paradoxically there is often something to learn about the future by looking at what we have experienced in the past. With this in mind, I will sketch some of the events and attitudes which have punctuated 10 years of work with child abuse in England.

In the early 1970s, society was at a stage where 'new' phenomena such as wife and baby battering, the increased prevalence of rape and maltreatment of children, were appearing more in the public eye. The feminist movement helped to publicise the exploitation of women and children by a powerful, male dominated society. From the mid seventies through to the early eighties this began to impact upon our thinking about sexist behaviour and discrimination against women. There was therefore a context of concern about inequality, and about the abuse of vulnerable individuals.

In 1980 and during the years which followed, information from the United States about the prevalence of child sexual abuse arrived in England, and the first cases of sexual abuse mostly of teenage girls, were seen by professionals. It is postulated that the attitude of society at this time (the early eighties) was one of hopelessness about the new problem.

A period of victim blaming and disbelief followed, so that victims were perceived as scapegoats for the abuse – the 'she asked for it' mentality. However, media coverage of child abuse was positive and proactive at this point, providing a vehicle for some individual child victims to be given a voice. In this way, a few articulate victims became accepted as credible, giving increased credibility to the increasing numbers of victims being identified.

Around 1982–3 pioneering treatment programmes such as the Great Ormond Street programme were dealing with small groups of families where sexual abuse had occurred. The peculiar family dynamics which seemed to involve denial of the process by all family members, and a great tendency to regroup when professional intervention ceased, were initially described. This model was elaborated using family systems theory, and in the mid 1980s the role of individual family members was further described but with little emphasis on the role of the perpetrator in instigating the abuse.

By the mid 1980s, the mother was often seen as some kind of scapegoat for the whole process of sexual abuse as having 'let it happen'. In the years to follow, however, more individual male and female victims spoke out both in therapy and in the media. It became apparent that many mothers within families where abuse had occurred were themselves victims, and an increasing sense of sympathy for victims and abused mothers developed. Around the same time, in 1986, victims began to be recognised as sufferers from post traumatic stress disorder (PTSD) and professional groups became, albeit reluctantly, involved in studying victim symptomology and offering treatment. The issues raised by the re-definition of victims as survivors, coupled with the resilience of victims and mothers in coping with long term abuse seemed positively to reframe the mother's position. This was a feature of work in the second part of the 1980s and resulted in the focusing of considerable anger towards abusers, as the abuser's true position in the family became more apparent.

Around 1988 work from America coincided with the limited work going on in England in relation to abusers, and confirmed that the process of abuse was far more calculated than casual; abuser's strategies and the cycle of deviant sexual fantasies within the mind of the abuser were more clearly described. At this point the abuser was seen not only as taking all the responsibility for the abuse, which was fair enough, but also as the scapegoat and the source of the whole problem. This in turn led many people to feel that incarceration, or even castration might, after all, be the only solution.

In the last year or so, however, further studies have revealed that many abusers were themselves the victims of child sexual abuse or other adverse experiences in childhood. The link between abusers as victims and the subsequent development of victims into abusers has become even clearer. Sad though this is, it has at least advanced our thinking to a point where we may feel more urgency to explore ways forward and approaches to the treatment of children as abusers.

Moving from the experience of the last ten years, it seems helpful to identify future issues as follows:

- The need for clear definitions in relation to child sexual abuse. This problem is a major challenge in relation to research methodology since different definitions of, for instance, 'sibling abuse' and 'sexual experimentation' between children of approximately the same ages, can result in vastly different prevalence estimates. Definition or confusion of definition extends to medical signs as well as to psychiatric sequelae, and some consensus is essential on these matters if the extent of abuse by children of other children is to be documented.

- The issue of 'normal' sexuality and how we define this as a society is something which has not been addressed in any consistent way in relation to child sexual abuse. If treatment of abusers involves, in part, cognitive work to change sexual fantasies which we deem to be deviant and unacceptable, that is, fantasies towards children and fantasies with a high sadistic, violent element, then it is essential that we have some base line information about the prevalence of such fantasies in the population as a whole. For instance, a recent survey by *Cosmopolitan* magazine of the views of readers about pornography made links between child sexual abuse, the rape of woman, and the use of pornography by abusers. Although the survey claims that female reactions to pornography were overwhelmingly negative, nevertheless one third of respondents found pornography sexually arousing. It is clear that a significant proportion of adult women share an aroused response to pornographic images of women and children in a way which is not openly acknowledged when we as professionals assume that all deviant sexual fantasies about children are harboured by men.

  A study by Briere and Runtz (1989) has also indicated that 22% of adult male college students experience attraction to children, with 5% masturbating to sexual fantasies about children, and 7% admitting they would abuse children if they could get away with it. This sort of research indicates that deviant fantasies involving children may be far more widespread than we have previously realised, and in order to inform our treatment initiatives with sexual abusers, it is important that more is learned about this subject.

- The issue of what constitutes 'abnormal' sexuality is also something which requires further investigation. Claims for the legitimisation of prostitution and pornography become more vocal in the light of the legal situation in other EC states. But, as professionals, we are well aware that problems of sexual adjustment may result in bisexuality, homosexuality and frigidity. We are also aware that these, as well as more extreme expressions of sexuality such as sado-masochism and bestiality, may all be possible sequels of child sexual abuse. The question may therefore arise as to whether these preferences or behaviours should be seen as resulting from informed choice by adults within a range of acceptable human sexual behaviours, or alternatively should be seen as symptoms or problems resulting from sexual abuse in childhood. Much more open debate may be needed about these issues before we can make headway with treatment for sexual abusers.

- In relation to treatment models at this stage, 10 years after the recognition of the problem of sexual abuse in the UK, no single approach to treatment of the abuser seems able to offer all the answers. The cognitive behavioural model may have the most to offer at present, but when working with teenage sexual abusers against children, it will also be essential to develop models which take on board the developmental needs of these children and include a component of family work.

- Long term follow up of young sexual abusers of children will show how effective treatment has been, and issues such as recidivism, adjustment to subsequent marriage, and parenting skills will need to be measured, in addition to looking at personal change during therapy.

- Indicators shown by children who are sexual abusers of other children, of their treatability, their dangerousness and the extent of their sexual deviance, need to be sought urgently from those engaged in treatment work. Such indicators can highlight which children should be targeted for treatment in the community, as opposed to the hopefully small numbers of children who may need containment in an institution.

- Resources for treatment include buildings, such as national or regional residential units, district based day centres along with staff resources such as care staff, therapy staff, supervisors and managers.

- Training is essential if children as abusers are to be picked out, protected and treated in an appropriate way. Training programmes for professionals need to be multidisciplinary, focusing both on general awareness of sexual offending behaviour, and also on specific therapeutic skills in working with such offenders.

Finally, although funding to support such treatment initiatives is urgently needed, it is important to point out that the major resource is the professional willingness to engage in this unpopular and difficult work. It is vital that colleagues in the helping professions such as psychiatry, probation and social services are specifically lobbied to become involved in setting up treatment projects for this work. For many years we have managed to avoid the subject of sexual abuse; the victims, the mothers, the consequences, and most of all the sexual offenders. Instead of allowing sexual offenders to continue to target children for abuse, we need to turn the tables and target sexual offenders for effective treatment.

Children as abusers: where are we starting from?

■

ANNE HOLLOWS

This chapter is based on reports from some of the group proceedings at the Children as Abusers Conference in March 1990. It sets out the experience of some 80 practitioners, from a wide range of professional settings, in working with children who have abused other children. It does not have the status of a survey in terms of methodological accuracy although we have taken pains to avoid generalising from the many particular examples quoted in the workshops. It is reported here to give an indication of the range of experience – and something of the flavour – of the state of the art as far as ordinary practitioners in health, social work and education are concerned.

There were two lengthy group sessions at the conference. The first, reported in this chapter, invited participants to reflect on their experience of work in the field to date; to assess the implications, for them personally and professionally, of their work in this field; to assess the impact on their agency; and to consider the wider locality context in which they were operating. In the second session groups addressed the issues which would be most helpful in moving their work forward.

The issues raised under each of the headings in the first session revealed much common ground. Issues of denial in all its complexity, the conflict between responding to a victim and to a victimiser; attitudes to the criminal justice system; the need for good supervision and management; and for better inter agency liaison recurred throughout each segment of almost every group's discussions. In preparing for the conference, we had identified a set of issues for each group to consider, at least in the initial stages of the group meeting. There was a measure of agreement that the headings offered a clarity of focus in an area where they had little experience of rational process. This chapter follows those headings.

Before describing the view from the field as explained in the group sessions several points should be stressed. The subject of children and young people as abusers was not new to the participants at the conference. Some of the people who came to the conference were struggling with their first case of a child abusing other children. Many others were reflecting upon considerable personal and agency experience in dealing with the problem. It should, be noted however, that almost all the cases discussed related to the upper end of the age range.

That many participants felt their work went unrecognised and unsupported was all the more disconcerting when the scale of incidence was shared. At the same time, their own experience of dealing with denial by colleagues and managers suggests that the scale of incidence known to the participants was almost certainly a substantial underestimate of the scale of the problem as a whole. Perhaps one of the most significant features of working in this field is the fact that any existing weaknesses or inadequacies in individual or collective responses to child abuse in general are thrown into stark relief. This in turn often leads to a greater anxiety in tackling the subject. Management systems and training programmes which do not fully prepare staff or organisations for dealing with child abuse, particularly sexual abuse, will have great difficulty in facing up to the complex challenge posed when the abuser is a child.

Personal issues

People who work with children who have been abused are regularly faced with the need to respond to a variety of conflicting emotions. For most people, the key personal issue is the constant dilemma of responding to the abuser as a child, usually in the context of work alongside other children. The nature of this dilemma is qualified by the age of the abusing child: responses to a very young child would differ from those towards a teenager.

Participants spoke of the constant pressure of providing care for needy youngsters while remembering that some of them were abusers. Work in this area combines three particularly fraught dimensions: work with victims of abuse, work with perpetrators of abuse and work with adolescents. This last dimension throws the others into perspective; it demonstrates the distinction between this work and work with adult perpetrators. Notions of morality and responsibility amongst adolescents are not fully developed – indeed many adolescents would see themselves as experimenting in behaviour generally. The conflict between responding to a needy child and dealing with the child who is behaving badly is common to work with adolescents. Some workers recognise, but others do not, the danger of moving between a punitive response and a response which tends to play down – even to minimise the abuse.

Our own responses

Our own experience of abuse

Much has been written about the problems faced by practitioners who have themselves been sexually abused and who find themselves working with abused children. Almost all of us have experienced some form of abuse, and if we can recollect it and our responses to it, we may begin to understand something of the traumatic stress described by Arnon Bentovim. Denial of our own abuse and the abusive behaviour which tends to result can only create problems for us as individual and often isolated professionals. Ironically, the problems could be turned to advantage if we harnessed our experience and started to integrate it into our present self-awareness.

Explaining our interest in the area of work

Many people reported on the comments which had been made by colleagues and managers regarding their interest in this area of work. While this was a feature of comments from professionals in several disciplines, it seemed to be most prevalent within social services. Not content with failing to support the work, managers mocked it in ways which seriously undermined the professional integrity of individual staff. Some participants commented that defensive responses, when asked to explain or justify our interest in this area of work, effectively compounded the problem. At the same time there was a recognition that it was not always easy to explain interest in the work, and many felt that in the current context of denial and disinterest it was important to be able to explain their interest in and commitment to the work in this area.

Gender and sexuality

There are undoubtedly assumptions and values, relating both to the behaviour of boys and male adolescents and also to girls, which serve to cloud the issue of child and adolescent abusers. The macho behaviour of even quite young boys receives barely concealed approval from older men (and women too) and this is often the case where the macho behaviour involves a degree of sexualised behaviour which may be abusive to some degree. Even young adolescent males who have committed quite violent sexual acts will receive a mixture of responses from adult males, some of which at least are favourable. At the same time girls are, from an early age, encouraged by many to take up sexualised roles. A common response from participants was that of rage and frustration at the sexualisation of children encouraged by advertising and by the use of children in adult television. Most participants agreed that these feelings should be acknowledged and respected. The significant numbers of girls whose inappropriate behaviour has become abusive to other children has had the effect of challenging existing thinking about the nature and causation of sexual abuse.

Power

Power and its abuse are features not only in the life and professional experience of practitioners. They are also often a feature of life within the establishments where children and young people who abuse spend much of their life. In particular, some schools and residential establishments may tolerate situations where abuse of power becomes a major feature in the culture of the establishment.

Issues about our own knowledge and understanding

Basic training

The recognition that a child is behaving in an abusive way is often difficult. It often takes place when the child is in a residential or day care setting (including schools) where both formal and informal contacts with other children and adults occur. The behaviour is therefore often recognised by staff whose own basic training in child sexual abuse is limited or non-existent. For many staff in residential settings access to in-service training is given a low priority. Although there has been widespread development of training for work with children who have been abused in local authorities, the staff group dealing constantly with many of the children who are abused are least likely to have had access to such training. Participants described stumbling across information; desperately trying to inform themselves from any available sources of information; and often tackling their own learning in a random way.

Knowledge of appropriate behaviour

Many of us have values, attitudes and assumptions which may encourage us to make judgements and responses to sexualised behaviour. Where these values and assumptions are based on mistaken premises, the judgements and responses will be wrong. Exercises where acts are ranked for perceived abusive content indicate the diversity of understanding of normal behaviour. There is a great need for wider knowledge and understanding of normal sexual behaviour at different age ranges. It would be helpful to have more knowledge of studies in this field.

Knowledge of child development

Associated with the above point was the generally felt view that outside of psychiatry and psychology, knowledge of child development, and in particular the range of behaviours and skills normal within an age band, was limited. There was also, particularly among social workers, a recognition that they often lacked any formal experience and training in developmentally appropriate direct work with children.

Issues as professionals

The overwhelming problem for professionals was felt to be the fundamental lack of knowledge at every level of the profession. This created for some a circle of denial which was difficult to break. In many agencies, both staff and managers have as yet, only a limited understanding of child sexual abuse. Theories of causation are poorly developed and understanding of appropriate responses is consequently limited. Particularly in residential settings, participants were aware of 'knee jerk' responses against a backcloth of real anxiety about accusations against staff themselves.

Professionals are increasingly aware of their inexperience in recognising and responding to this problem. As frontline knowledge and understanding develop, the lack of understanding and experience among many members of agency management is highlighted. Many of the participants felt that this was almost certainly responsible for the denial and/or minimisation of the problem at a management level. They spoke of management responses such as 'he will grow out of it' when the problem of an abusing child or young person was raised. In some settings where managers with minimal knowledge had begun to address the issue they had made crude generalisations in the opposite direction: 'that child is abused and soon he will become an abuser'.

Participants recorded the anxiety felt by professionals who are essentially motivated to help children and who have to face the reality that some children are very dangerous. To date, little work with children who have been sexually abused has involved close contact with the abuser, and the personal and professional consequences are substantial. There are difficulties too in adapting to the fact that children who abuse may well have moral systems which are in some ways lacking or skewed.

The overwhelming denial of the problem by managers takes two fairly distinct forms. The first is a direct form of denial which minimises the behaviour or dismisses it altogether. The second is less direct, with managers paying lip service to recognition of the problem but offering no resources or support to deal with it, forcing the child or adolescent to be responded to under some other, more acceptable heading. This is often compounded by variable levels of understanding between organisations which can effectively put a damper on any emerging understanding in a single agency.

Professional structures offer little to support work with children and young people who abuse. One participant described their agency as 'punitive in its failure to support and encourage work in this area'. Another drew attention to the tendency to respond to unknown situations by devising a heavily procedure based culture. This was felt to be inimical to the careful exploration of a situation where the child was the abuser because often the only identified client of the social services department was the victim. Others spoke of the difficulty in getting a formal case conference after abusing incidents involving young abusers. Participants wanted to see greater recognition of the problem within their agencies, greater staff support, supervision and access to consultancy in some cases.

Participants were concerned that, as yet, there had been little achieved in the creation of realistic resources to support their work with children and young people who abuse. Few were aware of therapeutic resources; even less had access to clearly defined residential resources. Many of those present were just coping, as best they could, with little access to specialist help. Some participants came from specialist units or therapeutic communities where there was a more creative and supportive approach to tackling the problem.

Summary

All of the foregoing comments build up to provide a dismal summary of the current professional response:

- What are the priorities and choices in style of work when working with abusers or working with victims? Where can we obtain information and specialist training in skills? Where can we find specialist resources if we ourselves are not competent or comfortable in this work?
- Many of the participants shared in the view that work with adolescents is often experienced to be one of the most difficult professional challenges. What they found hard to unravel was the extent to which this work is an extension of that challenge, and the extent to which it was an additional but separate challenge. Because of denial at all levels in the past, we are responding to adolescents who are abusers but who also come with a history of inappropriate responses from educational and residential care

settings. Many also have a history of breakdown and failure in placements. What do we tackle first in our response to the individual?

- The sort of history which many adolescents who are also abusers trail behind them, often as a consequence of our failure to recognise and respond appropriately to their needs, is not one which engenders sympathy in agencies hard pressed for resources. Where resource managers are not familiar with the issues it is often difficult to persuade them of the need to pay for expensive and possibly unproven therapy for those who have already had so much, albeit inappropriate, in terms of time and resources.

- Justice requires attention is also paid to the victim of the child abuser's acts – how can we achieve this? What potential is offered within the Children Act 1989 for the provision of therapeutic services to victims who may not fall within the conventional child protection procedures? Will resources be made available to meet these needs? How do we work with parents and families to encourage them to take up opportunities for such help where no family member has been involved in the abuse? Is there scope for work involving the victim with the victimiser?

- How does an agency support individual professionals who move into this area of work? Some innovative projects may be scorned while others are treated, at best, with mild interest. A further group of activities may be treated as a flagship, but usually only after they have managed to demonstrate some success. Some participants had watched reactions to their work move through all these stages, finally seeing the credit taken by the very managers who had scorned and neglected their efforts. How do we get agencies to take on board their responsibilities towards staff working in this area?

- Participants shared concerns about the appropriateness of different legal settings as a framework for intervention. Some saw the criminal process as offering a necessary opportunity for realistic acceptance of responsibility and therefore preferred the criminal justice route. But the harsher aspects of many judicial responses were also seen as leading to a tendency to minimise the offence. The criminal justice route has the consequence of labelling the abuser as a Schedule 1 offender. This was seen as both positive and negative, providing not only the opportunity to 'track' the future careers of young abusers, but also labelling them and seriously affecting many aspects of their life in the future. The civil court, through care proceedings, may be of value in some cases. It could offer the opportunity to underpin any therapeutic package with an element of compulsion, particularly where residence was concerned. How significant are the messages which we give to young abusers by our choice of process? How can we address the need for greater sensitivity and understanding among police, the judiciary and lawyers?

Issues for our agencies

There is inevitably a degree of overlap between the position of the individual professional, bounded as she or he will be by agency policies and procedures, and the agency as a whole. This section of responses tries to concentrate on the issues where agencies might offer policy development initiatives which could support work in this field.

There is often little understanding of the conflicts inherent in attempting to control abusive behaviour while at the same time offering care to the abused child. This is reflected in the unwillingness to resource treatment and therapy initiatives for abusing or 'offending' children at, for example, therapeutic communities. As a result many inappropriate placements are made, such as placing abusers in residential units with children who have already been abused.

The complicated consequences of failing at an agency level to recognise this area of work need to be demonstrated. A failure to recognise that children and young people may abuse others can result in:

- limiting the perspectives of those who investigate child abuse;
- failing to provide therapeutic intervention for all children who have been abused;
- failing to prepare staff who work with children from the youngest to the oldest to recognise abusive behaviour for what it is;
- failing to have records or statistics of the problem;
- failing to alert carers and parents to the existence of the problem;
- failing to develop inter-agency strategies to respond;
- failing to support staff who are trying to work in the field;
- failing to recognise that children can be so dangerous and need so much help.

Most fundamentally, by failing to recognise and respond to the problem, agencies are failing in their long term duty to protect children.

Issues for our locality

Discussions under this heading reflected the lack of any formally coordinated local response. This was identified as leading to 'territorialism' between agencies. In terms of planning packages of services for individual children, this could lead to continual passing of responsibility from agency to agency. The role of the Area Child Protection Committee was identified as essential to achieving development of locally based agreements for services. Participants reported little helpful activity at this level to date. There were, however, some accounts of positive informal activities at a local level. These centred on inter-agency support groups and service development groups. It was clear that a proactive local forum, with delegated authority to develop and link services, was an essential component of moving thinking forward – both within and between agencies.

Children as abusers: what could we achieve?

■

ANNE HOLLOWS

This chapter contains reports from the second set of group sessions held at the conference. During these sessions groups were asked to consider the attitudes, values and services which they would like to move towards in order to work effectively with children who have abused other children. The discussion which took place within groups ranged from the identification of detailed, practical proposals for action, to the consideration of the general principles which should underpin the formulation of policies. Some groups worked out the frameworks for responding to, for example, the accommodation options for abusing children or the supervision requirements of staff. Others wrestled with the relative merits of applying justice models or care models to children. Many of the group leaders reported on the strong sense of cooperation and collaboration among the range of agencies and professional disciplines who were represented within each group. This is significant in the context of accounts of current inter-agency conflict which many had reported from their own localities.

The clear outcomes of these group sessions are to be found in the recommendations detailed in the report of the final session, in the next chapter. This chapter highlights some of the debates from the groups which form the backcloth to the recommendations which they helped to frame.

The first, vital step towards the future requires a sharing of belief systems and practical approaches which reflect strong and purposeful management which is able to recognise and build on the practice of experience in the field. This needs to take place within all the agencies concerned. Only when individual agencies have a shared perspective and value base can they begin to take the next step of sharing at an inter-agency level. As with all inter-agency work, each agency needs to be clear about its own role and responsibility. The alternative is to allow this area of work to get caught up in existing conflicts within and between agencies.

At the same time it is clear that there will be a degree of overlap in the development of policies within and between agencies. The issue of 'who does what' will vary from area to area, depending on what sort of services are already in place and what may be developed. This means that all the agencies involved in the development of services in this area need to contribute to the collection of a common base of information, beliefs and resources. They also all need to share a commitment to working on the issue. Participants were anxious, however, to ensure that the outcome of the 'who does what' statement should not be a set of rigid demarcation lines drawn between staff and agencies. They saw a need to develop agency policies which were enabling, but where quality support and supervision would protect individual staff from working beyond their own capacities. Organisational frameworks which encourage flexible strategies were seen as essential to meet the needs of this client group. At the same time, the flexibility had to be within a system of known and respected boundaries. It was essential that the organisational framework ensured that staff were protected and enabled to do their best work.

Many of the groups reflected on the need for supported work which would explore cause and look at responses. For many organisations this would require something of a culture shift, a movement towards encouraging and enabling rigorous monitoring and local research projects. These research monitoring projects could, ideally, be linked to national initiatives to build a clearer picture of incidence and resources to meet different needs.

Recognition and guidance were sought at a national level in a number of areas. This particularly related to the issues around prosecution or diversion; care or control. Some participants felt that the Children Act 1989 offered the potential for developing a better response whereas others felt that clearly spelled out guidance on process were required. A possible consequence of national recognition of the problem was seen to be the provision of resources, although many participants questioned the value of such resources being channelled into a small number of centres of excellence.

In spite of an acute awareness of the difficulties and dangers of working in this area, no-one suggested that they were reluctant to continue. On the contrary, the message was clear that the wide range of professionals already engaged in the field were enthusiastic about continuing, providing that they had opportunities to communicate about their work, and providing also that they had access to identified sources of expertise and consultancy, to avoid the dangers of 'burn out' and maintain their own impartiality.

Turning to some of the more specific proposals developed in the groups, there was a common thread of anxiety about how to provide age appropriate living environments for children who posed a risk to other children. The tension between enabling children who had abused others to share in educational, leisure and family living experiences while protecting vulnerable children was, for many participants, unresolved. The importance of extending knowledge and skills among a wide range of professionals and volunteers working with children was stressed. In particular, issues of confidentiality and the danger of collusion were brought to the fore.

Groups identified the need to have access to a range of resources for accommodation. These would include carefully selected and prepared alternative family carers as well as residential and therapeutic settings. Natural families could also be supported as on-going parents where they were able to manage the risk to other children in the family. Decisions about accommodation would need to reflect the outcomes of a detailed assessment of the child, with reference to both their status as victim and as victimiser.

In therapeutic terms it was felt important to look at the potential for avoiding a separation between the abuser and the abused. Joint work could be undertaken in some circumstances and there was American experience to draw upon. This joint work could include the using of video material of the victim, to empower the victim to confront the abuser.

The role of parents in therapeutic work was also suggested as an important option to consider. They must be involved in understanding why abuse happens and their understanding may, in turn, provide a considerable support for therapeutic intervention.

The importance of developing a variety of therapeutic models and skills was emphasised. It was felt that the key issue of which model to use for which circumstance would then be able to be more realistically addressed by multidisciplinary teams.

There is a need for all the professionals involved to understand that others may be able to offer help, education and training in work in this field. In connection with the abuser, there is much more information and research needed to understand the family setting and dynamics, and to develop frameworks for treating the abuser both in society and in the context in which they have abused. There was an acknowledgment that an important precondition for building the future pattern of services would be a greater public awareness of the issue. Opinions about how to achieve this were divided: a tension which was continued in the final session of the conference. Some felt that careful and gradual exposure of the problem was likely to achieve a supportive public response: other favoured a major media initiative.

Most of the discussions which took place in the group were able to contribute to the agenda setting activity of the final session. Some of the specific steps to be undertaken in order to meet these targets for the future are addressed in the concluding chapter of this publication, 'An agenda for action'.

The group discussions achieved another end too. This was partly to do with a recognition by individuals of the 'art of the possible': providing an opportunity to share information about local initiatives and to develop the confidence to move forward. The groups also provided an opportunity to progress from the feelings of isolation and, in some cases, despair which had characterised some of the earlier discussions.

Conclusion: the agenda for action

■

ANNE HOLLOWS

This chapter is based on the final plenary session of the conference, which attempted to draw together the threads of the workshop sessions by identifying key issues for the future direction of work with child and adolescent abusers.

In a sense the seminar itself provided the first step towards progress in this work for the 80 people who attended it. At an individual level, contacts were made and ideas exchanged which provided an immediate support for developing work. At a collective level, by putting the issues 'on the map', the seminar helped to move towards a certain level of professional and public acknowledgement that children and adolescents could themselves engage in sexually abusive behaviour. But participants agreed that recognition was only the first step towards developing practice and support for work with these young people. The following points have been brought together as a summary of the most pressing concerns for work in this field at the present time.

1. Sharing experience of practice

Many of the people who attended the seminar stressed the need for better coordination and sharing of information about practice experience. They also sought greater sharing of ideas, and knowledge about developments in the field of working with children and young people as abusers. It was recognised that this had been the concept behind the seminar, but it was also stressed that attendance at the seminar reflected only a small number of those who were currently involved in the work. There was a clear desire for regular opportunities for wider sharing of knowledge and experience in this area of work.

This sharing of experience is needed at a number of levels. First, there is a need to provide some kind of network of information, easily accessible by workers across all the disciplines who might be involved in this work. This would enable them to access sources of further information as well as identifying resources to assist with their work. Second, the need for a coordinated information base also implies a sharing of values and policies between all the services who may be involved with working with children who abuse. Each individual agency engaged in this area of work needs sufficient understanding of the work, throughout the management chain, to develop clear policy guidelines which reflect an understanding of the tensions. Only then will individual agencies be in a position to move forward to share their policies and values with other agencies.

2. Management of the work

It is important to develop management approaches which reflect the specific needs of children and young people who abuse, while at the same time retaining the overall context of work with children and young people. The development of such approaches will require managers and supervisors to have a familiarity with the issues and tensions inherent in the work, an understanding which is rarely found at the present time.

It is also important to identify the roles, responsibilities, potential and limitations of the different professionals engaged in this work. Many participants recognised the danger of territorialism developing between different professional groups. The need to capitalise on joint training initiatives which have been fostered both by child protection training and in preparation for the Children Act's implementation will be crucial. This would enable psychiatrists, social workers and judges to begin to expand their own understanding of this kind of offending and its early symptoms.

In addition there may well be a need to recognise the specific skills and knowledge which should be a requirement for work in this area, identifying those who are working with children who are abusing other children, so that they can be seen as distinct specialists. Most people feel that this area of work is different enough to warrant distinction both from general offender work and from victim work.

This leads to the need to establish some kind of boundaries between protection work and offender programmes. Children need to benefit from a multi-agency approach which can recognise their own needs for child protection as well as recognising their offender behaviour. It is important to include in this the need for assessment and treatment work, and appropriate settings for this to take place for the child.

3. The legal context

There is need for clarity about the statutory and legal context of abusing children. Many professionals have considerable difficulty in perceiving that a child can be dangerous to other children and it is important to make sure that this is properly recognised. There needs also to be some clarity as to whether and when treatment for children who abuse should be voluntary or set in a firm legal framework. Here again, there is a need to incorporate both the police and the judiciary into discussions. There is no doubt of the need for greater knowledge among these groups of the early indicators of abusive behaviour. Arnon Bentovim's paper has referred to research which details early behaviour patterns pointing towards the development of sexually abusive behaviour, and this needs to be understood so that children and young people showing the first signs of such behaviour can receive treatment as soon as possible.

4. The role of the Area Child Protection Committee

Area Child Protection Committees are in an ideal position to put the issues on the agenda at a local level and to set the pace for joint strategies to respond at a number of levels. First they have the potential to gather together information on the scale of the problem in a particular area. They are well placed to extend knowledge of the issue among the different agencies involved and to develop training initiatives. In addition, they can make plans for a coordinated response in their area to young children who abuse and monitor the impact of coordinated interventions. It is also important to recognise that ACPCs have a duty to address the issue of prevention. In this area of work prevention is effectively going to mean an early response, through assessment and treatment strategies, to each abused child. This will aim to ensure that that child is helped to avoid developing behaviour patterns which may damage other children.

At the present time Area Child Protection Committees have no formal framework for sharing their experience one with another. This is urgently required if there is to be the ability to learn from different kinds of experience in this area of work.

5. Prevention, education and the media

There is considerable concern about how to deal with this subject in the wider community and media context. While some would argue for a gradual and careful exposure of the problem, others would suggest that the full scale of the issue – and the dilemmas of the response – should be exposed. Media attention to child abuse is considerable but the particular issues associated with children who abuse have received scant attention in contrast with the coverage of so-called ritual and satanic abuse. What is required is a media response which is factual, well-informed and generates a demand for better therapeutic intervention at an early stage with abusing children.

The general public should be aware that children who have been abused may themselves begin to abuse others. This should not seek to further victimise the abused child but to develop more public accountability for those who are responsible for planning the treatment and response to children who are abused.

One of the few education representatives at the seminar pointed out afterwards the need to train and use teachers and schools to recognise early indicators of abusive behaviour. She said schools should develop strategies with children to protect themselves from abuse by other children as well as adults. It was pointed out that response within schools is crucial and schools may themselves be able to offer insights into treatment, drawn from their experience of responding to bullying.

6. Who gets the most attention?

In child abuse there is always a victim and a victimiser. Childcare workers in any discipline have a clear responsibility to give paramountcy to the child's welfare. But in this work, both victims and victimisers are children and with scarce resources where do the priorities lie?

Many of the victimisers will themselves be the untreated victims of abuse – sometimes abuse which only comes to light through their victimising behaviour. We need to understand how to balance the conflicting demands and the different phases of intervention so that issues of protection, prevention and therapy can be covered effectively.

7. Management

It is important to use every opportunity to address managers within all the disciplines involved in and concerned about this subject area. There is considerable evidence of denial amongst senior managers in social services, health, police, and other disciplines. It will be important for professional agencies to take on board these issues. Only when managers can begin to recognise the issue will they begin to act upon all the points in this agenda.

8. Agencies and denial

Denial is not just limited to managers but may exist more widely within agencies, limiting individual and group ability to accept any information about children who abuse. The attitudes towards staff working in this area and the widespread reported disinterest in innovative projects are two examples. More insidious is the way in which denial can permeate an agency's culture, inhibiting access to training, staff development, information and resources.

9. Power and gender

It was widely felt that agencies have barely begun to confront the issues of the abuse of power and of gender stereotyping. This can be demonstrated, for example, in the low attention paid either to the training and staff development of workers in residential settings or to realistic preparation for foster carers. It can also be demonstrated in the ambivalent attitudes to sexual experimentation among children whom the local authority is looking after. The importance of respecting individual differences in personal values and standards vies with the need to have a common frame of reference for activities which are detrimental to others. Participants agreed that this was one of the 'overarching issues' which are far from being resolved in agencies and society in general but felt that the issue was an essential feature of forward thinking in developing an effective response.

10. The problem of accommodation planning

One of the most pressing practical issues raised by participants was that of accommodation strategies for children and young people who abuse others. Hair-raising reports of innappropriate placements were widespread. The long-standing denial of the problem for many young people had led to them being inappropriately, and usually unsuccessfully, placed in residential establishments where a number of the children would be the vulnerable victims of other people's abuse. Breakdowns in fostering and residential placements only added to the difficulties in responding to and treating such young people. It was agreed, in feedback from several groups, that foster care with carefully prepared and supported carers could offer a lot to young abusers. It might certainly offer less risk of them being in contact with younger, vulnerable children. There was no doubt, however, that considerable experience and support would need to be given to carers taking on such a task.

Residential placements pose no less a challenge, although it is in some respects a different challenge. The importance of a culture of openess and clarity among staff in such establishments could not be overstated, along with clear channels of support and training. The need to devise follow-on placements with a measure of watchfulness over the longer term outcomes for young abusers was also recognised.

In summary, participants wanted each area to have a strategy for assessment and placement of children in settings which combined therapeutic work with a measure of protection for other children. It was clear that each strategy would need to include a range of placement options, backed by support and guidance for staff and carers.

11. Creating clarity between mainstream work with adolescents and work with children as abusers

This issue was raised first in the context of general staff development issues, to flag up the importance of setting the work in an age appropriate context. It was also raised because of its implications for decision-making about which agency bears the lead responsibility in a case. Abusive behaviour, particularly among adolescents, is often seen as requiring adult-oriented intervention. There is no doubt that in this work there is a case for close links to be made between social services departments and the probation service, but packages of services will need to incorporate age appropriate experiences and involve workers with experience of relating to younger children.

12. Development of written agreements between agencies

It was felt that much of the work in this area would involve several disciplines, often from more than one agency. Because it would be essential to have absolute clarity about responsibilities and to ensure against weak links in the chain, it was suggested that written agreements should specify how key staff involved in multi-agency, multi-disciplinary work may be supported.

13. Need to develop a joint approach to perpetrators under the framework of 'Working Together'

The revision of *Working Together*, the Department of Health's Guidance on multidisciplinary working in child protection, to incorporate the changes introduced in the Children Act 1989, was identified as a major opportunity for developing advice and guidance on work with children who abuse.

14. Moving forward: the response of each agency in a multi-agency framework

It was generally agreed that the quality of the multi-agency response would be directly related to the extent to which the individual participating agencies had agreed a clear framework for activity in respect of children and young people as abusers. While some of the processes involved in reaching this position would be personal and internal to the organisation – dependent upon the quality and ability of agencies to work towards resolving issues at these levels – there would be some external influences, including the recognition and accessibility of relevant research. A further crucial issue in moving agency and inter-agency research forward was seen as being the availability of resources to do the work. The availability of resources might perhaps be an incentive to enable quite a lot of difficult thinking and personal work to be undertaken, but it would also make that work worthwhile rather than leaving expectations unfulfilled.

At an agency level there was a lot of concern that current inconsistencies in practice and response could only be overcome by developing good 'inter' and 'intra' agency policies so that each agency was quite clear about its own role and its own responsibilities, and so that the potential for workers getting caught up in existing conflicts within and between agencies would be minimised.

15. The need for supported work which can explore cause and look at response

Under this heading the first and most crucial issue is for agencies to listen to workers and to be prepared to offer a supportive response to make and share definitions and belief systems. This would ultimately lead to the development of much better 'in-house' research and quality control in dealing with the problem.

The second issue is the acknowledgement that each agency has a role which may be different but is, nevertheless, a part of the whole picture of working with children. An example of what this means is found in the issue of training. Training for all professional groups involved in this area should enable them to map the particular part they are able to play in dealing with the issue so, for example, the courts need training about the early behaviour of abusing children, so that it can be appropriately dealt with. Social services departments need to understand the particular recognition and investigation issues in dealing with the problem. In short, there is a need for an acceptance of models for dealing with child abusers which are multi-dimensional and deal with the different facets of that information. In order to achieve this there is a need for much greater information and understanding about our notions of child protection, risk, responsibility, and dangerousness; notions which are different when we are dealing with children from those in operation when we are dealing with adult abusers. It is particularly important to understand these concepts where the child who has been abusing is kept in the community.

This leads to the third issue: the development of organisational frameworks which encourage flexible strategies. These frameworks will require some high level support, in particular from the Department of Health and from ACPCs, for whom this issue should be identified as a current agenda topic. More widely, the role of teachers and youth workers is also crucial. ACPCs should be able to provide an effective local forum for feeding in ideas and information and indeed should be a platform for demanding and overseeing a coherent professional response. In this way the work done by individual agencies can be brought together, concentrating on the commonalities rather than on the negatives and exclusivities. This will facilitate consideration of the provision of systems and packages of services for an individual.

Summing up the closing session of the day, Valerie Howarth, Director of ChildLine, said that much of what had been shared at the conference were old issues on new territory. Pointing out the lack of opportunity within our culture and educational experience to debate our sexuality and where we come from, she felt that real prevention could only emanate from that sort of process – and real prevention is effectively the only lasting means to child protection. There must be a widespread public recognition of the need for treatment of the victim, the abuser, and the abuser as victim.

References

These references relate specifically to the chapter developed by Arnon Bentovim, but, in addition, provide a good current reading list.

Abel G.G. and Becker J.V. 'Sexual Cognition Scale'. 1985. Reproduced in Salter A.C., *Treating Child Sexual Offenders and Victims*. Sage: London: 1988.

Abel G.G., Becker J.V., Mittelman M., Cunningham-Rathier J., Rouleau J. and Murphy W., 'Self Reported Sex Crimes in Non Incarcerated Paraphilias'. *Journal of Interpersonal Violence*, 2(1), 3–25: 1987.

Abel G.G., Mittleman M.S. and Becker J.V., 'Sex Offenders: Results of Assessment and Recommendations for Treatment' in: Ben-Aron H.H., Hucker S.I. and Webster C.D. *Criminal Criminology*. M.M. Graphics, Toronto: 1985.

Ageton S.S., *Sexual Assault Amongst Adolescents*. Lexington Books: 1983.

Baker A.W. and Duncan S.P., 'Child Sexual Abuse: A Study of Prevalence in Great Britain'. *Child Abuse and Neglect*, 9, 457–467: 1985.

Becker J.V., 'The Effects of Child Sexual Abuse on Adolescent Sexual Offenders' in: Wyatt G.E. and Powell E.J., *Lasting Effects of Sexual Abuse*. Sage: Beverley Hills: 1988.

Becker J.V. and Able G.G., *Methodological and Ethical Issues in Evaluating and Treating Adolescent Offenders*. U.S. Department Health and Human Services: 1985.

Bentovim A., Boston P. and Van Elburg A., 'Child Sexual Abuse – Children and Families Referred to a Treatment Project and the Effects of Intervention'. *British Medical Journal*, 295, 1453–1457: 1987.

Bentovim A., Elton A., Hildebrand J., Tranter, M. and Vizard E., *Child Sexual Abuse Within the Family: Assessment and Treatment*. Butterworth: London: 1988.

Bentovim A. and Kinston W., 'Focal Family Therapy' in: Gurman A. and Kniskern D., (eds) *Handbook of Family Therapy*. Basic Books: New York: 1991.

Bentovim A. and Ratner H., 'Focal Family Therapy with the Family of an Adolescent Offender' in: Friedrich W., (ed) *Case Studies of Sexual Abuse*. Norton: New York: 1991.

Briere J. and Runtz M., 'Post Sexual Abuse Trauma' in: Wyatt E.G. and Powell E.J. *Lasting Effects of Child Sexual Abuse*. Sage: Beverley Hills: 1989.

Brown E.J., Flanagan T.J. and McLeod M., (eds) *Sourcebook of Criminal Justice Statistics – 1983*. Washington D.C. Bureau of Justice Statistics: 1989.

Buss A.H. and Durkee A., 'An Inventory for Assessing Different Kinds of Hostility'. *Journal of Consulting Psychology*, 21, 343–349: 1957.

Cantwell H.B., 'Child Sexual Abuse: Very Young Perpetrators'. *Child Abuse and Neglect*, 12, 579–582: 1988.

Cardoza M. and Hamblion M., *A Group for Adolescent Offenders*. 1990.

Chasnoff M.D., Burns W.J., Schnoll S.H., Burns K., Chisum G. and Kyle-Spore L., 'Maternal-neonatal Incest'. *American Journal Orthopsychiatry*, 56, 577–580: 1986.

Davis G.E. and Leitenberg H., 'Adolescent Sex Offenders'. *Psychological Bulletin*, 101, 417–427: 1987.
De Jong A.R., 'Sexual Interreaction Among Siblings and Cousins: Experimentation or Exploitation?' *Child Abuse and Neglect*, 13, 271–279: 1989.
Fehrenbach P.A., Smith W., Monastersky C. and Deisher R.W., 'Adolescent Sexual Offenders: Offender and Offence characteristics'. *American Journal of Orthopsychiatry*, 56, 225–233: 1986.
Fehrenbach P.A. and Monastersky C., 'Characteristics of Female Adolescent Sexual Offenders'. *American Journal of Orthopsychiatry*, 58, 148–151: 1988.
Finkelhor D., *Sexually Victimised Children*. Free Press: New York: 1979.
Finkelhor D., 'Four Preconditions: A Model' in: Finkelhor D., *Child Sexual Abuse: New Theory and Research*. Free Press: New York: 1984.
Finkelhor D. and Browne A., 'Initial and Longterm Effects: A Conceptual Framework' in: Finkelhor D. *A Source Book on Child Sexual Abuse*. Sage: Beverley Hills: 1986.
Friedrich W.N., 'Behaviour Problems in Sexually Abused Children: An Adaptational Perspective' in: Wyatt G.E. and Powell E.J., (eds) *Lasting Effects of Child Sexual Abuse*. Sage: Beverley Hills: 1986.
Gebhard P., Gagnon J., Pomeroy W. and Christenson C., *Sex Offenders: An Analysis of Types*. Harper and Rowe: New York: 1965.
Glasgow D., 'Children and Adolescents Who Commit Sexual Offences'. Presentation to Institute of Child Health: 1990.
Henggler S., *Delinquency in Adolescence*. Sage: 1989.
Johnson T.C., 'Female Child Perpetrators – Children Who Molest Other Children: Preliminary Findings'. *Child Abuse and Neglect*, 12, 219–229: 1988.
Johnson T.C., 'Female Child Perpetrators: Children Who Molest Other Children'. *Child Abuse and Neglect*, 13, 571–585: 1989.
Johnson T.C. and Berry, 'Children Who Molest.' *Journal of Interpersonal Violence*, 4, 185–203: 1989.
Kavoussi R.J., Kaplan M. and Becker J.V., 'Psychiatric Diagnoses in Adolescent Sex Offenders'. *Journal of the American Academy of Child and Adolescent Psychiatry*, 27, 241–243: 1988.
Kempe C.H., 'Recent Developments in the Field of Child Abuse'. *Child Abuse and Neglect*, 3, ix–xv: 1979.
Knopp F.H., *Remedial Intervention in Adolescent Sex Offences: Nine Programme Description*. Safer Society Press: Syracuse: 1982.
Lloyd and Walmsley, 'Changes in Rape Offences, Sentencing'. *Home Office Research Report*, HMSO, 105: 1989.
Longo R.E., 'Sexual Learning and Experiences Amongst Adolescent Sexual Offenders'. *International Journal of Offender Therapy and Comparative Criminology*, 27, 150–155: 1982.
Madanes C., 'Systemic Approaches to Adolescent Offenders and Families'. Presentation to Institute of Family Therapy, London: 1989.
McLeer S.V., Deblinger E., Atkins M.S., Foa E.B. and Ralphe D.L., 'Posttraumatic Stress Disorder in Sexually Abused Children'. *Journal of the American Academy of Child and Adolescent Psychiatry*, 27, 650–654: 1988.

Mrazek P.B., Lynch M. and Bentovim A., 'Recognition of Child Sexual Abuse' in: Mrazek P.B. and Kempe C.H. *Sexually Abused Children and Their Families*. Pergamon Press: 1981.

Pierce L.H. and Pierce R.L., 'Adolescent/Sibling Incest Perpetrators' in: Horton H.L., Johnson B.L., Roundy L.M. and Williams D., (eds) *The Incest Perpetrator*. Sage: California: 1990.

Pomeroy J.C., Behar D. and Stewart M.A., 'Abnormal Sexual Behaviour in Prepubescent Children'. *British Journal of Psychiatry*, 138, 119–125: 1981.

Pynoos R.S. and Eth S., *Post-traumatic Stress Disorder in Children*. American Psychiatric Association: Los Angeles: 1985.

Rosenfeld A.A., Bailey R., Siegel B. and Bailey G., 'Determining Incestuous Contact Between Parent and Child: Frequency of Child Touching Parents' Genitals in a Non-clinical Population'. *Journal of the American Academy of Child Psychiatry*, 25, 481–484: 1986.

Rosenfeld A.A., Siegel B. and Bailey G., 'Familial Bathing Patterns: Implications For Cases of Alleged Molestation and for Pediatric Practice'. *Pediatrics*, 79, 224–229: 1987.

Russell D.E.H., 'Sexual Exploitation'. Sage: California: 1984.

Ryan G., 'An Annotated Bibliography: Adolescent Perpetrators of Sexual Molestation of Children'. *Child Abuse and Neglect*, 10, 125–132: 1986.

Ryan G., 'Victim to Victimiser'. *Journal of Interpersonal Violence*, 4, 325–341: 1989.

Ryan G., Lane S., Davis J. and Isaac C., 'Juvenile Sex Offenders: Development and Correction'. *Child Abuse and Neglect*, 11, 385–395: 1987.

Salter A.C., *Treating Child Sex Offenders and Their Victims: Practical Guide*. Sage: Beverley Hills: 1988.

Schecter M.D. and Roberge L., 'Sexual Exploitation' in: Helfer R. and Kemp C.H., (eds) *Child Abuse and Neglect: The Family in the Community*. Ballinger: Cambridge, Mass: 1976.

Smith H. and Israel E., 'Sibling Incest: A Study of the Dynamics of 25 Cases'. *Child Abuse and Neglect*, 11, 101–108: 1987.

Smith M. and Grocke M., *Self-concepts and Cognitions About Sexuality in Abused and Non-abused Children: An Experimental Study* (in preparation).

Smith W. and Montastersky C., 'Assessing Juvenile Sex Offenders Risk of Re-offending'. *Criminal Justice and Behaviour*, 13, 115–140: 1986.

Wilson G., *The Secrets of Sexual Fantasy*. London: 1978.

Yates A., 'Children Eroticised by Incest'. *American Journal of the American Academy of Child and Adolescent Psychiatry*, 27, 254–257: 1982.

Wyre R., *Working With Sex Offenders*. Gracewell Clinic: 1989.

Index

E, F

G, H

I, J, K

L, M

N, O, P

Q, R

S, T

U, V, W

X, Y, Z